INTELLIGENCE

Stuart Ritchie

ALL THAT MATTERS

First published in Great Britain in 2015 by John Murray Learning. An Hachette UK company.

First published in US in 2015 by The McGraw-Hill Companies, Inc.

This edition published in 2015 by John Murray Learning

British Library Cataloguing in Publication Data: a catalogue record for this title is available from the British Library.

Library of Congress Catalog Card Number: on file.

Paperback ISBN 978 1 444 79187 7

eBook ISBNs 978 1 444 79180 8; 978 1 444 79179 2

1

Typeset by Cenveo® Publisher Services.

Printed and bound in Great Britain by CPI Group (UK) Ltd., Croydon, CR0 4YY.

John Murray Learning policy is to use papers that are natural, renewable and recyclable products and made from wood grown in sustainable forests. The logging and manufacturing processes are expected to conform to the environmental regulations of the country of origin.

John Murray Learning
Carmelite House
50 Victoria Embankment
London
EC4Y 0DZ
www.hodder.co.uk

For my parents

Contents

About the author

Dr Stuart J. Ritchie is a postdoctoral research fellow at the Centre for Cognitive Ageing and Cognitive Epidemiology in The University of Edinburgh's Department of Psychology. His research focuses on how intelligence develops and changes across the lifespan, what might influence it in childhood, and how we might prevent it from declining in later life. His studies of intelligence have been published in journals such as *Psychological Science*, *Current Biology*, *Child Development* and *Intelligence*.

Acknowledgements

As luck would have it, I know some very smart people who have helped immensely with this book. I'm grateful to George Miller for suggesting I try my hand at writing it, and to Edinburgh Skeptics for hosting my first talk on intelligence, which formed an outline for the topics discussed here. Iva Čukić, Ian Deary, Katharine Atkinson and Andrew Sabisky all made extremely useful comments on earlier drafts, and during the writing I benefited greatly from discussions with Rogier Kievit, Michael Story and Tim Bates, among many others. Any less-than-intelligent errors in the book are mine alone.

All the graphs in the book were made by the author, using Hadley Wickham's 'ggplot2' package in R. I thank Mark Bastin for providing the brain image in Figure 4.3.

1

Introducing intelligence

'There is... an unusually high and consistent correlation between the stupidity of a given person and [their] propensity to be impressed by the measurement of IQ.'

Christopher Hitchens, The Nation

Smart people don't like the idea of intelligence. Just mention 'IQ' in polite company, and you'll be informed (sometimes rather sternly) that IQ tests don't measure anything real, and reflect only how good you are at doing IQ tests; that they ignore important things like 'multiple intelligences' and 'emotional intelligence'; and that those who are interested in intelligence testing must be elitists, or perhaps something more sinister.

But anyone who makes these arguments simply hasn't seen the scientific evidence. The research shows that intelligence test scores are meaningful and useful; that they relate to education, occupation and even health; that they are genetically influenced; and that they are linked to aspects of the brain. Studies of intelligence and IQ are regularly published by psychologists, neuroscientists, geneticists, psychiatrists and sociologists in the world's top scientific journals. *Pace* Christopher Hitchens (see previous page), we really should be impressed with the measurement of IQ. The purpose of this book is to give an up-to-date summary of the modern science of intelligence, and answer the common questions that are asked about it. We'll start off with the most obvious question of all...

▶ What is intelligence?

Sceptics of intelligence research often make their opening gambit by asking this deceptively simple question: 'How do you even *define* intelligence?' The implication is that, if researchers can't give a snappy definition of intelligence, they can't possibly claim to measure it using IQ tests. Here is one attempt at a definition (Gottfredson, 1997):

> Intelligence is a very general mental capability that, among other things, involves the ability to reason, plan, solve problems, think abstractly, comprehend complex ideas, learn quickly, and learn from experience. It is not merely book-learning, a narrow academic skill, or test-taking smarts. Rather, it reflects a broader and deeper capability for comprehending our surroundings, 'catching on', 'making sense' of things, or 'figuring out' what to do.

OK, not particularly snappy. But it would be surprising if something as complicated as human intelligence could be summed up in a brief soundbite. The definition above describes a mental capacity that everyone has to a degree, but what's crucial for our discussion in this book is that not everyone has the same capacity: *some people are more intelligent than others*. It's these intelligence differences that are studied in most IQ research, and that are noticed in schools, in workplaces, and in everyday life.

▶ A potted history of intelligence testing

It took a surprisingly long time for people to think about measuring differences in intelligence. It's not as if intelligence is a new concept: notably smart people have been written about since at least the ancient Greeks (consider, for instance, what set Odysseus apart from the other mythological heroes). Philosophers have discussed human faculties for centuries. One popular conception, attributed to Aristotle, was the 'five wits': imagination, fantasy, memory, reason and the 'common sense'. These were mentioned by Aquinas in the thirteenth century, Chaucer in the fourteenth and Shakespeare in the sixteenth; some of them were hazily analogous to what scientists would now consider 'cognition' (see Deary, 2000, for some other historical examples). Again, though, for a remarkably long time, little thought was given to how one might *measure* the differences between people in these attributes.

The psychologist Arthur Jensen (1998) suggested two reasons for this. The first is that rationality was often seen as something divine that could only fleetingly be tapped into by humans: if reason was a gift from God, it didn't make sense to try to measure it. The second is that, until relatively recently, few people were formally schooled; education is the context where intelligence differences are most in evidence, and if only a privileged few attended school, there wasn't much opportunity to notice – or to consider measuring – these differences.

It may be no coincidence, then, that the mid-to-late nineteenth century, which saw compulsory education laws introduced across Europe, was the period where testing intelligence was first seriously considered. Perhaps appropriately, the first steps were made by a true genius: Charles Darwin's half-cousin, Sir Francis Galton (Figure 1.1).

▲ Figure 1.1 Sir Francis Galton (1822–1911) 'in middle life'. (Plate lxi from K. Pearson, 1914.)

'Polymath' doesn't even begin to cut it with Galton: it's hard to exaggerate the sheer variety (and, sometimes, eccentricity) of the contributions he made to human knowledge. He invented indispensible statistical concepts (two of which are discussed below), as well as the science of fingerprinting, weather maps, the dog whistle, and the idea of 'crowdsourcing'; he even had time to explore and map previously unknown parts of Africa. Fascinated with measuring and enumerating everything it was possible to measure and enumerate – from the levels of boredom displayed by the tilting heads of students in his colleagues' lectures, to the relative attractiveness of women on the streets of various British cities (London came first, and Aberdeen came last, in case you're wondering) – Galton began to reflect on 'eminence'. What was it that made some people rise to the top in society? Why did some families seem to have many eminent individuals while others had none?

In attempting to answer these questions, Galton weighed up the effects of socialization and heredity, and coined the phrase 'nature and nurture' (we'll get to the genetics of intelligence in Chapter 4). He wondered whether there was some kind of test people could take that would indicate whether they would go on to achieve eminence. In 1884 Galton set up an 'Anthropometric Laboratory' at the South Kensington Museum in London to try out some possibilities for this test. He collected, within a year, vast amounts of data on over 9,300 visitors: their social class, their physical measurements, their reaction times (measured using an contraption involving a swinging pendulum), and their abilities to discriminate between visual and auditory stimuli (Johnson et al., 1985). His idea, to 'effectually "sample" a man with reasonable completeness' (Galton, 1908) was vastly ahead of its time, but he didn't go much further with the data.

That job fell to the psychologist James McKeen Cattell (1860–1944), who in the 1890s designed a set of sensory tests that he thought might reveal something about a person's fundamental thinking skills. Unfortunately for Cattell, the particular tests he used appeared to have little relation to his participants' educational achievement, and this line of enquiry was shelved.

The first true intelligence tests came not from studying eminent individuals with the highest ability levels, but instead those at the bottom of the distribution. In 1904 the psychologist Alfred Binet (1857–1911) was tasked by the French government with creating a tool to identify children with what we'd now call learning disabilities: children who would need special educational attention. Binet wanted something that wasn't subjective like psychiatrists' reports, and something that could group children into different levels of disability.

With his collaborator, Théodore Simon (1872–1961), Binet set about creating a selection of different mental tasks that he believed children of each disability level could perform. The levels were named, in order of decreasing ability, with the now-offensive titles 'débile' (or 'moron'), 'imbécile', and 'idiot'. For example, Binet believed that 'idiots' would be able to follow the movement of a lit match with their eyes, but wouldn't be able to name objects pointed at by an examiner. 'Imbéciles' would be able to repeat back relatively long sentences, but wouldn't be able to define abstract terms like 'boredom' (Nicolas et al., 2013). In later revisions of the test, Binet had the insight of attaching ages to each of the levels, so that the examiner could tell whether a child was developing normally, or was lagging behind the ability level expected for their age.

The terminology – 'idiots', 'imbéciles' and the rest – makes all this sound terribly harsh, but Binet's writings reveal a very humane attitude: after all, his tests were designed so that each child would get the additional education they deserved. He also thought that, with extra input from teachers, children could progress upwards and improve their abilities. To this day, educational psychologists routinely use intelligence tests to identify children who might struggle in school.

Once Binet had set the groundwork, it wasn't long before other researchers began to apply the tests in different contexts (Fancher, 1985). Psychologist Lewis Terman (1877–1956) returned to Galton's original purpose, attempting to find children who scored particularly well on the tests, and follow them through life (we'll discuss the lives of those with very high intelligence in Chapter 3). Terman also added many more tasks and questions of higher difficulty to Binet's test, and was the first to use the abbreviation 'IQ' for 'Intelligence Quotient'. During the First World War, the Harvard psychologist Robert Yerkes (1876–1956) designed tests that could be administered to groups of people, rather than individually. These were used to screen new recruits for the US Army, and assess their appropriateness for officer-level positions. An example of the kind of task required in one of Yerkes's army tests is shown in Figure 1.2. Armed forces across the world still regularly use intelligence tests for new recruits; later in the book, we'll see that some very useful samples of intelligence testing data have been collected from countries where there's compulsory military service.

When it came to understanding what intelligence actually is, the most important early contributions were made by the British psychologist Charles Spearman (1863-1945). Like Galton, Spearman was a statistical innovator, inventing mathematical techniques now in everyday use by scientists in many fields. Spearman's

▲ Figure 1.2 A 'picture completion' test item from Yerkes's *Group Examination Beta*, a test of intelligence for illiterate army recruits. The task is to notice what's missing from the picture. (Yerkes, 1921.)

most famous idea was that, in contrast to what had been thought previously – Binet, for instance, considered there to be separate mental abilities – there is in fact such a thing as 'general intelligence', a property that causes people to perform well on a multitude of different cognitive tests. I won't say too much about Spearman here: we'll get the verdict of modern research on his ideas in Chapter 2, which discusses general intelligence and the debate Spearman had over it with another IQ research pioneer, Sir Godfrey Thomson (1881–1955).

In the UK of the early twentieth century, psychologists like Thomson were concerned most of all with education. Thomson, along with his contemporary Sir Cyril Burt (1883–1971), was worried that the British educational system allowed too many talented children from the working classes to languish in deprived schools, and worked on applying intelligence testing to identify them. This is not to say that Burt and Thomson weren't interested in helping children of lower ability: Thomson wrote in 1942 that 'the same amount should be spent on each individual during his lifetime, disregarding entirely both his needs and his abilities' (Deary, 2013). The idea was that each child would receive the appropriate education for his or her intellectual level.

Thomson and Burt influenced the British government's passage of the 1944 Butler Education Act, which established grammar schools, where children who got a high enough IQ score on a test at age 11 (the '11-plus') would go to learn a complex curriculum including Classics and mathematics. Children with lower scores on the 11-plus would attend technical or 'secondary modern' schools, to learn less advanced materials. This system, which has a controversial legacy, is no longer in operation in the UK, which now mostly has comprehensive schools. We'll discuss educational selection again in Chapter 6, and we'll look at the complicated connection between intelligence and education from numerous angles throughout the book.

Hanging over all of this early research, from the very start, was the spectre of eugenics. The idea that we should selectively 'breed' humans to produce healthier, smarter future generations – either by encouraging people in higher social classes to have more children ('positive eugenics'), or by discouraging the lower classes from reproducing ('negative eugenics') – was a preoccupation of large numbers of progressive, liberal thinkers in the late nineteenth and early twentieth centuries. The intelligence research pioneers (except for Binet, who appears to have had little interest in the subject) were no exception: indeed, Francis Galton invented the term 'eugenics' in the first place.

It's reasonable to be appalled at the results of the eugenics movement. One such result, forced sterilization of those deemed 'feeble-minded', was policy in the US, Canada, all the Scandinavian countries, and others, both before and for decades after the horrors of the Nazi genocide in Germany. Intelligence tests – though of a very perfunctory manner – played a part in these programmes, although they were by no means necessary for them: sterilization policies were active well before the psychologist Henry Goddard (1866–1957) suggested using Binet's tests for eugenic purposes in the early 1910s. In any case, we must separate out the political beliefs of these early researchers from any facts they discovered about human psychology. Facts, after all, have no necessary moral or policy implications: it is up to us to decide what to do about them once they are discovered.

▶ Intelligence: all that matters

In the rest of the book, we'll see how the foundations of intelligence research laid by figures like Galton, Binet, and Spearman have been built upon by modern science. We'll start, in Chapter 2, by looking through a set of tasks you could expect to complete if you sat an IQ test today. How does a person's performance on one task relate to performance on the others? To what extent was Spearman correct about 'general intelligence'? Then, in Chapter 3, we'll see how IQ test results relate to how people do in school, at work and in life more generally. Chapter 4 goes 'under the hood' to look at the biology of intelligence: how it might have evolved, how it relates to genetics, and what a smarter person's brain looks like. Chapter 5 asks whether we might be able to improve intelligence and make people brighter. Do 'brain training' games work? What about education?

The final chapter, Chapter 6, asks why, if there's all this scientific evidence backing it up, intelligence is still so controversial. In the historical sketch above, I mentioned a couple of reasons, but the discomfort with intelligence testing goes deeper than just revulsion at its history: it touches on profound political and moral issues about equality. By the end of Chapter 6, I should have convinced you that, despite the controversy, intelligence research is a vital scientific field.

▶ Some notes on statistics and terminology

Two statistical concepts will pop up regularly in this book, and it's worth outlining them before we start. The first is **correlation**. One of Francis Galton's most enduring inventions, correlation is a way of quantifying the strength of the relation (the 'co-relation') between two 'variables' (a variable is just anything that can be measured).

Take parent and offspring height as an example. We know that taller parents are very likely to have taller children, and we also know that there are some exceptions to this rule. In statistical terminology, we'd say that there's a 'strong positive correlation' between parent and offspring height: 'strong' because of the high likelihood of finding tall parents with tall children (but not 'perfect', which would imply that taller parents *always* have tall children); 'positive' because as one variable (parental height) increases, the other variable (offspring height) tends to increase, too (if one variable decreased as the other increased, the correlation would be 'negative'). Correlations are sometimes referred to as 'associations', 'links', 'relations', or, if one variable precedes the other in time, 'predictions', but these all refer to the same thing.

Galton created a statistical formula that puts numbers on these correlations, indexing the strength of the relation. The numbers range from −1.00, a perfect negative correlation, to 1.00, a perfect positive correlation. The closer to 1.00 (or −1.00 for negative correlations), the stronger is the relation. A correlation of zero indicates no relation between the variables whatsoever. The italicized letter *r* is used to denote a correlation, and you'll see this many times throughout the book (in the form '*r* = 0.50'). The following diagrams illustrate a variety of correlation strengths in the form of scatterplots (which are, incidentally, a type of graph that Galton partly invented).

It's common to hear that 'correlation does not equal causation', and you should bear this in mind as we

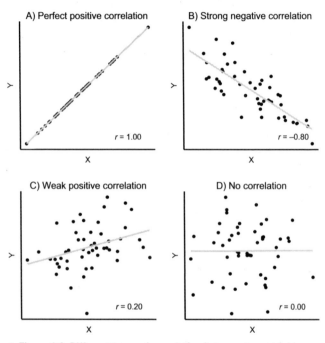

▲ Figure 1.3 Different types of correlation between two variables, 'X' and 'Y'. The grey lines are summaries of the strength of each association: the steeper the line, the stronger the correlation. In A), the perfect positive correlation, values of X can be precisely predicted from values of Y. This almost never occurs in reality. In B), there is a strong negative correlation: as X increases, Y is very likely to decrease. In C), there is a weak correlation: X and Y are related, but not strongly. In D), X is completely unrelated to Y, and thus the summary line is flat.

discuss the many correlations that have been found involving intelligence test scores. For instance, if intelligence and educational achievement are correlated, this might mean (a) that intelligence causes you to do better in school, (b) that schooling helps you do better on intelligence tests, (c) that something else, perhaps social background, causes you to do better at school and on intelligence tests, or (d) a mixture of all the above. Nevertheless, we shouldn't forget that a correlation does sometimes *imply* causation: it's difficult to think of any instances of causation where there's no correlation.

A step more complicated than correlation is **regression**, a statistical technique that allows us to look at a correlation between two variables while simultaneously 'controlling for' others (or, to put it another way, 'holding other variables constant'). For example, maybe you think that social background is the explanation of the intelligence–education relationship. Regression allows you take social background into account, and thus to ask: 'If everyone had exactly the same social class, would there still be a correlation between intelligence and educational achievement?' We'll see the answer to this specific question later in the book, but the idea of controlling for variables will appear a few times in different contexts.

Finally, a note on terminology. This book focuses on **differential psychology**: the study of differences between people's mental characteristics. For that reason, when I talk about 'intelligence' (or 'smartness', or 'cleverness'), I won't mean 'the property that all humans have, but that all rocks don't'. Usually, I'll mean 'differences between people as measured using intelligence tests'. Once you've seen the evidence I'll present, you can decide whether this definition relates to the one given at the start of the chapter, or to more popular conceptions of 'intelligence'.

2

Testing intelligence

'VLADIMIR: I don't understand.

ESTRAGON: Use your intelligence, can't you?

[Vladimir uses his intelligence.]

VLADIMIR: [finally] I remain in the dark.'

Samuel Beckett, Waiting for Godot

How do we measure how smart someone is? This chapter describes an intelligence test, and how each part of it measures a different mental ability. We'll then look at how these abilities are related, and discuss the most ubiquitous finding in all of intelligence research: general intelligence, or the '*g*-factor'. Then we'll consider how intelligence changes across the lifespan (spoiler: if you're over 25, it's not good news).

▶ A modern intelligence test

Let's imagine you were having your intelligence tested today. We'll look at a few of the sorts of tasks (or 'subtests') that you might be asked to do. Before we start, it's worth pointing out that a full, reliable intelligence test can take rather a long time – often well over an hour – and should be given by an expert examiner. Some shorter IQ tests exist for when researchers want to test large numbers of people, but beware online tests that claim to provide your IQ after a ten-minute set of puzzles: they bear little relation to real intelligence tests and are usually pretty worthless. Many of the kinds of tests described below were first designed by David Wechsler (1896–1981), another intelligence testing pioneer. Updated versions of his tests, which were first published in 1955, are still in regular use today.

Let's start our IQ test with an assessment of your **reasoning** ability. Look at the patterns in Figure 2.1.

Which of the options A–F at the bottom comes next in each sequence? These are two examples of the test known as 'matrix reasoning'. There is a 'matrix' of pictures with a rule that governs their sequence, and it is your job to reason your way to the correct answer, completing the sequence from the available options. A full test would involve a few dozen of these puzzles, starting off with easy ones like number 1, progressing towards more difficult items like number 2. We might follow up the matrix task – which didn't involve any words or language – with some *verbal* reasoning. For that, we could ask you about 'similarities': What do 'honesty' and 'patience' have in common?

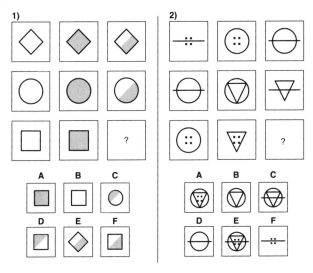

▲ Figure 2.1 Two 'matrix reasoning' test items (similar to those in real IQ tests, but created by the author). For each, which option from A–F correctly completes the sequence? Number 1 is very easy, but number 2 is much trickier.

Next, we'll test your **memory**. For one task, the examiner will read a list of numbers aloud (for example, 6-3-5-8-4), and you have to repeat them back from memory, but in reverse order. As this test, known as 'digit span', goes on, the lists of numbers become longer, challenging your ability to hold and manipulate information in a kind of short-term storage buffer that psychologists call 'working memory'. Some nastier versions of the task also include letters among the numbers, and ask you to repeat the numbers and letters in numerical and alphabetical order. There might also be a brief mental arithmetic test, which will also exercise your working memory. The examiner will then read you a story that's one or two paragraphs long. Afterwards, you'll have to answer a few questions on what happened in it, without being able to hear it again.

We now move on to **knowledge**. We'll first look at vocabulary, asking you to define each of a list of words, ranging from the commonplace (*advantageous*), to the obscure (*ebullient*), to the fiendish (*synecdoche*). While we're at it, we'll test your general knowledge, also with a set of ever-more-difficult questions. We might also throw in a test of 'verbal fluency': how many words can you think of in one minute that begin with the letter 'P'?

Your mental **processing speed** will be tested next. This can be measured in many different ways, but most commonly a paper-and-pencil test is used – you'll be asked to match up a set of symbols (that you've never seen before) to numbers or letters as quickly as you can, or to cross out one particular shape that's hidden among many others, also as fast as possible. Another test of speed is the reaction time test. How quickly can you move your finger from a set position to a button when a light comes on? This task can be made to test somewhat different mental skills by having multiple lights that turn on at random, meaning that you'll have to rapidly move your finger to any one of several locations (a task that is also substantially tougher than the single-light version).

And now – surprise! – we return to that short story you heard earlier. You'll now have to answer a new set of questions about the story, which will be tougher, since more time has passed since you heard it, and you've been distracted with all the other tests. Finally, the tester might administer a mental rotation task: they'll show you a selection of pictures of 3D shapes floating in space, and ask you to imagine rotating them by 180 degrees. You then have to match the results to a set of options. This is a test of **spatial** ability.

This concludes your intelligence test. The examiner can now calculate your IQ score. This is done by totalling up your performance on each test, then comparing your performance to that of others. We know how others have done because IQ test-makers (who, these days, are often large companies) trial the tests on huge, representative samples of people, in order to create 'norms'. Whatever the average score of the 'norming' sample is, it's converted to an arbitrary value of 100 to make things simpler: this number represents 'average

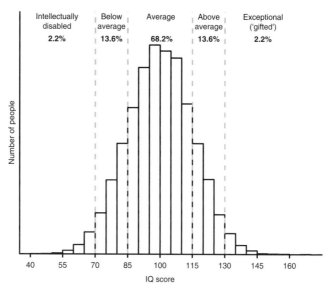

▲ Figure 2.2 How standardized IQ test results are distributed. Easy and difficult items are balanced so that most people get an average score (the highest bars), with few people with scores in the very high and very low ends of the distribution (the almost invisible bars at the extreme left and right). Along the top, the graph also shows the percentage of people who will fit into each category.

intelligence'. We can see in Figure 2.2 that the test–makers ensure that most people get IQ scores around the average, with fewer people getting very high scores (at the far right-hand side, indicating giftedness) and very low scores (at the far left-hand side, indicating learning disabilities): plotted this way, IQ test scores form a 'normal distribution', and drawing a continuous line around the scores gives the well-known 'bell curve'.

It's worth thinking about what would happen if you sat the same tests again in, say, a few weeks' time. IQ test-makers have considered this, and collect data using the norming samples on what's called the 'test-retest reliability' of their measures. That is, how consistent is someone's score across multiple sittings of the same test? Subtests are included in standardized IQ tests only if they are highly reliable, and correlations from session to session tend to be around $r = 0.80$. That's high, but it's not a perfect correlation. Scores will tend to vary across time (perhaps during one test you didn't try as hard as you possibly could, or were staring out of the window when the examiner asked you the question), but for each person multiple scores will cluster around their 'true' ability level. The more tests you take, the better idea you will have of what this 'true' ability is.

Bear in mind that the tests above are just a small selection from a vast number that have been used to measure intelligence through the years. Most full intelligence testing sessions will include at least some of these tasks, or at least very similar ones. There are also simpler tests aimed specifically at children.

At this point, you might be wondering whether the examiner is justified in adding up the scores from all these tests. Don't they all measure different things? If so, wouldn't taking a total be like adding apples and oranges, giving a meaningless result? In the next section, we'll answer this question by looking at one of the most important findings about intelligence: the *g*-factor.

'Gaming' the tests

A common criticism of IQ testing is that the tests don't actually measure anything fundamental about mental ability, but instead measure motivation, anxiety, or perhaps how much a person has previously practised. It has been found that increasing people's incentives to perform well by offering them a monetary reward somewhat improves IQ scores. However, the overall effects are small, and in many IQ-testing situations – for example college or workplace entrance exams – the stakes and incentives to perform well are very high anyway.

Can you 'game' an IQ test by practising it beforehand? Nobody would deny that, if you practise something, you get better at it. But IQ tests are designed to be used with the general population at large. Thankfully, most people don't spend large amounts of time practising IQ tests (they have better things to do). Also, some tests are easier to practise than others: a full IQ test with a wide range of different measures gets around all but the most committed pre-practice. Importantly, even if everyone practised the tests, there would still be differences in the speed it takes to learn them. This is what we might call intelligence.

▶ Nothing but a *g* thing?

We've seen that an IQ score is the total from a wide range of tests that all tap different mental skills and abilities. As you read through the descriptions of the tests, you might have pictured people you know who would, say, zip through the speed measures but would struggle with the puzzles shown in Figure 2.1. Or people who would ace the vocabulary test but – given their inability to add up the bill after dinner – would do terribly on arithmetic. Crucially, these people are exceptions to the rule. Contrary to many people's intuitions, it turns out that, to a great extent, *intelligence is general*. In other words, people who are good at one kind of mental test tend to be good at them all.

This is seen whenever a decent-sized sample of people sits a variety of tests like the ones above – the test scores will all correlate positively together. Charles Spearman, whom we encountered in the previous chapter, called this finding 'the positive manifold', and a century of research has confirmed he was correct. A comprehensive review by the psychometrician John Carroll (1993) showed that the positive manifold was found in every one of over 460 sets of intelligence testing data. Some researchers have even deliberately created cognitive tests tapping different skills that they expected not to correlate together, but they always did. The positive manifold of seemingly unrelated tests is one of the most well-replicated findings in psychological science.

It didn't have to be this way. It might have turned out that people who are excellent problem solvers are only so good because their skills in other areas have suffered: perhaps they have poorer memories because they have a 'reasoning' brain rather than a 'remembering' one. It might be that people who react quickly also tend to have poorer vocabularies. These scenarios are possible in theory, and would result in negative correlations between the scores on some cognitive tests. But they're

▲ Figure 2.3 Charles Spearman, the discoverer of the *g*-factor of intelligence, with a cup of tea. (Drs. Nicholas and Dorothy Cummings Center for the History of Psychology, University of Akron. Used with permission.)

not true in practice (see the following boxed text). It's worth stepping back for a moment and realizing how impressive this is – before we'd done the research, would we have predicted that people who are faster at moving their finger when a light blinks will be more likely to know the definition of *defenestrate*? Not necessarily. The positive manifold is remarkable, and it demands an explanation.

Multiple intelligences

In the 1980s the psychologist Howard Gardner argued that, instead of a general factor of intelligence, there are in fact multiple intelligences. These include 'linguistic' intelligence, 'logical-mathematical' intelligence, 'musical' intelligence, 'interpersonal' intelligence and 'bodily-kinaesthetic' intelligence. Since then, he has added 'existential', 'laser' and 'mental searchlight' intelligence to the list; there are now around ten in total. He argues that people differ on this whole range of intelligences, and that the intelligences don't necessarily correlate together.

There's just one problem with this theory: there's no evidence for it. Gardner just came up with the concept and added the additional intelligences seemingly on a whim. At no point did he gather any data, or design any tests, to support his idea. The notion of 'multiple intelligences' has become very popular among educators, as a kind of wishful thinking: if a child has poor (say) logical-mathematical abilities, the argument goes, they might still be good at another kind of intelligence! But denying the huge amount of evidence for general intelligence does nobody any favours. Many of Gardner's 'intelligences' can be conceptualized as skills, or even personality traits, but to describe them as 'intelligences' makes a mockery of the definition of the word. (See Waterhouse, 2006, for a detailed critique of multiple intelligences.)

This is where the *g*-factor comes in. Psychologists use a statistical technique called **factor analysis** to look for patterns in complicated data. Imagine we had made a large number of physical measurements of people who attended a gym: their muscle strength in their legs, arms and back; the time it takes them to run five kilometres; their lung capacity; their body mass index; and how many push-ups they can do in one go. Say we wanted to work out each person's overall fitness. Like the cognitive tests above, these fitness measures will all correlate positively together: people who can do more push-ups will tend to be able to run faster, have more powerful lungs, et cetera. The reason the measures correlate together might be that there is something shared between all of them – something that makes them generally high in one person and generally low in another. That something is what we might call 'fitness'. Factor analysis allows us to extract this shared aspect from the assortment of correlated measurements.

It works in exactly the same way for intelligence tests. All of the positively correlated IQ subtests described above have something in common, and this is what Spearman called the 'general factor of intelligence', the 'g-factor', or sometimes just 'g', for short. Spearman thought that no single subtest was a perfect measure of g, but that when factor analysis was used to isolate only what a range of subtests had in common, this gave an insight into a person's all-purpose intellectual power. Averaging across the wide variety of tests, the usual result is that differences on the g-factor explain around half of people's overall intellectual differences.

The g-factor gets everywhere – there are no cognitive tests that aren't linked to g at least to an extent – but it doesn't explain everything about mental abilities. Each particular test requires some specific skills (which Spearman called 's-factors') in addition to g. Some subtests measure more *g*, and some measure more *s*: the extent to which a subtest taps *g* is called its '*g*-loading'. Tests with strong *g*-loadings tend to be the ones involving complex thought, like matrix reasoning, or that reflect a lifetime of reading books, learning quickly from texts, and engaging intellectually, like vocabulary. Lower *g*-loadings are found for tests that are less demanding, like 'simple' reaction time tasks where the only requirement is a reaction to a single light.

Another remarkable thing is that *g* is found no matter which subtests you use. The psychologists Wendy Johnson, Thomas Bouchard and their colleagues (Johnson et al., 2008) have studied large samples of people who had been given several separate 'batteries' (or subsets) of IQ tests. Each battery contained entirely different tests, designed by different test-makers. Johnson and Bouchard extracted a *g*-factor from each battery, then looked to see how strongly the *g*s were related. The correlations were about as high as correlations can be: although found in entirely separate tests, these *g*-factors were essentially identical. The conclusion was that, regardless of how you test someone's intelligence, there's 'just one *g*'.

But what *is* the *g*-factor? Spearman proposed that *g* reflected something like 'mental energy': one single property of the brain that varied between people, reflected better or worse genetic make-up, and determined whether their test scores were generally high or low. This would be as if one single process, like muscle strength, were responsible for differences in all the fitness measures we discussed above. Some modern psychologists have followed in Spearman's footsteps, theorizing that processing speed might be the key to this mental energy. They argue that the brain's efficiency is at the root of all mental abilities: faster brains get more done in a brief time frame, and can thus pack in more operations (Jensen, 2006). We'll see how this idea, which is still far from proven, relates to the wiring of the brain in Chapter 4.

Other researchers have suggested that working memory, which we discussed above and which involves holding and working on information in short-term mental storage, might be the basic mechanism that underlies g. Being able to hold on to more information that needs to be dealt with (that is, having a higher-capacity working memory) is clearly an advantage for all kinds of cognitive tasks, so this idea makes intuitive sense. But, as with the speed theory, we don't yet have the right evidence to know whether working memory should have a privileged place in our explanation of the g-factor (Conway et al., 2003).

There are completely different ways of looking at g. Spearman's rival, the educational psychologist Godfrey Thomson, suggested that there doesn't need to be a single underlying property, like speed, that contributes to every single mental test. Thomson proposed that the brain performs many different basic processes (some examples might be 'addition', or 'noticing the similarity between a square and a rectangle'), and that these are differently 'sampled' by the various IQ subtests. Put simply, perhaps matrix reasoning samples one particular process, 'A', that's also sampled by mental rotation, and another, 'B', that's sampled by working memory; for their part, mental rotation and working memory both sample another process, 'C'. So long as there is this kind of overlap in the sampling of processes across the subtests, the subtests will correlate positively together (and a g-factor will appear), even if there isn't one fundamental process driving everything.

There is debate in psychology about whether Spearman or Thomson was correct about g; nobody has yet made the right discoveries to clinch the argument (Bartholomew et al., 2009). But this rather arcane and nerdy disagreement needn't distract us from the consensus: whatever its cause, there is a general factor of intelligence; comprehensive IQ tests measure it and, as we'll see in the next chapter, it matters.

▶ The substructure of intelligence

The fact that g exists, and is clearly important, doesn't mean that it's the only part of intelligence we should care about. Psychologists have also spent years working out the full substructure of intelligence tests, of which the general factor is only a part. In our gym analogy above, this is like seeing how the individual measurements group together at a lower level: even though everything is positively correlated with everything else, the measures of muscle strength, for example, will be particularly strongly related to each other.

For intelligence, you might think that this would just involve grouping together all the 'memory' tasks, the 'reasoning' tasks, the 'speed' tasks and so on, but it's not so simple. One of the most popular models splits general intelligence into two subgroupings, called 'fluid' and 'crystallized'. Fluid intelligence involves working things out on the basis of no previous knowledge. For example, the matrix reasoning test or the reaction time test can be given completely 'cold' – people don't need to use any prior experience to solve the puzzles or to react to the light. On the other hand, 'crystallized' intelligence is made up of the sorts of tests (like vocabulary and general knowledge) that rely on information gained outside the testing environment, in the real world. But alternative theories exist: for example, one view is that the tests are really grouped together into 'verbal', 'perceptual' and 'rotational' domains (Johnson and Bouchard, 2005). Arguments between psychologists over the substructure of intelligence show no signs of abating.

▶ Intelligence across the lifespan

There's one context where the fluid-crystallized distinction comes into its own: **cognitive ageing**. As you can see in Figure 2.4, which shows data taken from a set of tests given to a sample of more than 6,000 people of all ages, cognitive abilities ramp upwards in childhood. As children mature, they get better at problem solving (the dashed line showing fluid intelligence) and also

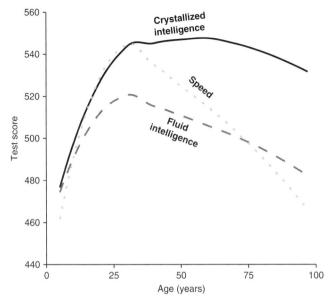

▲ Figure 2.4 Change in cognitive abilities with age, taken from a study testing over 6,000 people of all ages (the data for different ages come from different people). 'Fluid' skills (dashed line) decline far more steeply than 'crystallized' ones (solid line). Tests of speed (dotted line) show a particularly pronounced decline. (Figure adapted with permission from Tucker-Drob, 2009.)

more knowledgeable (the solid line showing crystallized intelligence; see the box below for one theory of the *g*-factor that relates to this period of life). But there's a clear distinction in what happens next. Crystallized abilities continue to rise for many years, as we accumulate more knowledge (this is perhaps what people mean when they talk about the 'wisdom of age'). But, rather depressingly, from around the mid-twenties, fluid intelligence declines, and continues to do so right into old age. I've also included a dotted line showing speed tests, to show that these have the steepest age-related decline. Ageing makes our brains more sluggish, and we progressively lose the ability to solve problems efficiently and hold new information in our working memories.

Mutualism

We've seen that Spearman and Thomson had differing theories on the meaning of the g-factor. More recently, the psychometrician Han van der Maas and his colleagues have proposed a third theory, called 'dynamic mutualism' (2006). This theory suggests that, when we are born, there is no g but simply lots of independent abilities. As we mature, though, the different abilities all piggyback on each other: perhaps speed helps working memory develop, while working memory acts as scaffolding for reasoning. The g-factor emerges from this web of 'mutual' interactions. The theory makes a clear prediction: that you won't find a g-factor in young children, but will in adults, where it has had time to develop. The initial evidence has not been kind – one recent paper found a strong g-factor in children as young as two years old (Gignac, 2014) – but it remains a fascinating and under-explored idea.

The decline in intelligence matters. It happens to people whether or not they go on to develop dementia. In later life, it's been linked to a drop in the ability to make important decisions and perform everyday tasks like reading labels, managing finances, and remembering to take medicines (Tucker-Drob, 2011). Most Western countries now have ageing populations, where people are working and living longer, and their governments are rightly concerned about how the resulting cognitive decline will affect their social and economic prospects. We know some people age better than others, though (the lines in Figure 2.3 are averages), so scientists are trying to learn the lessons of the healthy agers and apply them to those who decline more rapidly. A huge amount of research money is now being spent on finding ways to prevent or treat cognitive ageing. Make no mistake: this is intelligence research, and it's one of the most important areas of scientific investigation occurring today.

A few tentative results have emerged from the research on cognitive ageing. For example, it seems that encouraging older people to be more physically active can preserve their fluid intelligence (Lövdén et al., 2013). But the biggest predictor of being smarter in old age is rather obvious, and perhaps somewhat disheartening: being smarter in childhood. One unique study recently provided the best evidence on this. In 2013 the psychologist Ian Deary gave a sample of Scottish people aged 92 the exact same intelligence test that they'd all sat when they were 11 years old, in 1921. Even after all that time, there was an impressive correlation between the childhood and adult tests: r = 0.54 (illustrated in Figure 2.5). That is, people who did well on the test in childhood were likely to be sharper in old age: they experienced less decline in their abilities.

The evidence on the stability of intelligence tells us two things. First, whereas the correlation across the lifespan is quite strong, it is far from r = 1.00. Many of the reasons some people age better than others are not to do with their prior levels of intelligence: we just need to find

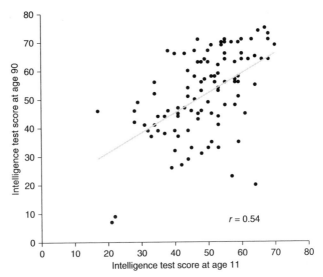

▲ Figure 2.5 The stability of intelligence across life. This shows the results of the same intelligence test given to the same people (one person per dot) at age 11 and again at age 90. There is a correlation of $r = 0.54$, shown by the grey summary line. (Data adapted from Deary et al., 2013, with permission from Sage.)

out what they are. Second, we might want to look at the period of life before that age-11 intelligence test, to see if we can boost intelligence in childhood. We'll discuss some potential means to do this in Chapter 5.

▶ Summary

There's no single way to assess someone's intelligence. We've seen that measures ranging from pattern-based puzzles to vocabulary quizzes, from reaction speed timers to memory tests, are all regularly used by psychologists. The most important fact is that, despite the sheer diversity of the tests, people doing better at one test usually do better at them all. This 'positive manifold' of test correlations gives rise to the general 'g-factor' of intelligence, which has a number of different interpretations – it might reflect the general speed of brain in performing all its tasks, or a more complicated interaction of many different basic abilities. To get a good measure of it, you need to give a wide variety of different cognitive tests. We've also seen that some – but not all – of the functions measured by intelligence tests show a precipitous decline as we get older. Young readers: make the most of it while it's there.

The nature and structure of mental abilities is an interesting question for scientists to ponder. But does any of this matter in the 'real world'? What's the practical importance of knowing someone's general intelligence? That's the topic of the next chapter.

PS: To put you out of your misery, the answers to the matrix reasoning items in Figure 2.1 are: 1F; 2B.

3

Why intelligence matters

'Perhaps our intelligence is not just ended by our mortality; to a great degree, it is our mortality.'

Adam Gopnik, The New Yorker

Smarter people live longer. In study after study, it's been found that people with higher IQ scores – and, thus, higher general intelligence – tend, on average, to outlive their less intelligent peers. In some studies, IQ score is about as predictive of the risk of death as is smoking. Why on earth would your score on the kind of tests we saw in the last chapter predict when you're going to die? As with so many scientific questions, the answer is complicated, and we'll have to follow several different threads to find it. In this chapter, we'll look at what intelligence tests can tell us about a person: their educational and job prospects, their health, and even their religious and political beliefs. Along the way, we'll piece together the reasons for the tests' impressive predictions about mortality.

▶ Education

Let's start with the sphere that's most obviously linked to intelligence: education. IQ test scores are strongly and unambiguously correlated with two different, though related, measures of education: achievement (that is, your exam results) and duration (that is, how long you stay at school, and whether you go on to college or university).

In one of the largest and most representative studies of education and intelligence to date, the psychologist Ian Deary took IQ scores from over 13,000 schoolchildren aged 11, and then tested how well they correlated with the children's achievement on their age-16 GCSEs (a set of standard school exams taken in England and Wales; Deary et al., 2007). The correlation between the g-factor of intelligence and an overall exam score was $r = 0.81$. This is a stunningly strong link – recall from Chapter 2 that the highest a correlation can be is 1.00. Correlations as high as the ones in Deary's study are almost unheard of in psychology. It means that whatever the exams were measuring, it was very close to what the IQ tests were measuring. Even more strikingly, the exams were measuring something close to what was tapped by the IQ tests *five years* earlier.

Hundreds of studies over the years have found the same link: IQ tests, taken early, predict who will get the highest exam results. In large part due to these exam results, higher-IQ people will tend to stay at school for longer and will be more likely to go on to get degrees and other qualifications. To some people, these results might be obvious. It's no surprise, they'd say, that people who IQ tests show to be fast learners would do well at school: after all, learning is what school is all about.

Others, though, bristle when they hear about these findings, and accuse the researchers of reducing all the complexity of education to something as simple as an IQ score. It's true that some caveats are required:

1 IQ is not *exactly* the same thing as educational achievement, and having a high IQ doesn't ensure educational success: see the box below for a discussion of psychological traits that are important in addition to intelligence.

2 We'll see in Chapter 5 that there might be effects going in the opposite direction, too: education might also improve intelligence.

3 These findings don't apply to people with specific learning disabilities. A range of conditions like dyslexia, dyscalculia and specific language impairment, which slow the development of particular skills, can impede educational progress even when general intelligence is high.

All that matters?

Intelligence is a major predictor of a whole host of outcomes. But it's by no means the only one. Take educational achievement. Being bright is critically important, but so are other characteristics like conscientiousness, motivation and self-control, as well as various social skills. Huge swathes of psychology research are devoted to understanding a range of personality characteristics, and these are often included in analyses alongside IQ, so that the relative contributions of both can be tested. It's been found that, for instance, motivation levels and intelligence both have their own separate predictive effects on school performance (Ritchie and Bates, 2013). The existence of these studies should instantly refute the silly but commonly heard criticism of IQ research that states: 'You can't sum up a person in a single number!' Nobody with any sense ever claimed you could.

But none of these provisos takes away from the impressively strong predictive power of intelligence tests in education. You'll have noticed that we've already begun to answer the question asked at the beginning of the chapter, of why higher intelligence predicts a later death. Not only will better-educated people be more aware of how to stay healthy, but more qualifications allow entry into better jobs, which bring all the health benefits that more income provides. The next section looks at jobs in more detail.

▶ Jobs and social class

If you're an employer, and you want to select workers for different positions in your company, you won't want to ignore intelligence. A huge number of scientific studies now attest to the fact that intelligence tests are predictive of performance in the workplace. They're predictive whether or not performance is measured by the monetary worth of a person's output, their efficiency on the job, or ratings by their managers. The tests are also predictive of how much employees will learn in work-related training, so if you want to keep your employees up to date with the latest skills, you'd be better off hiring people who score well on IQ tests.

Figure 3.1 shows the relations of IQ test scores to different aspects of work performance. As you can see, IQ scores are better indicators of performance in more complex jobs, but they do still predict how well people do in simpler ones. IQ is even positively – though more weakly – correlated with skills like leadership: on average, brighter people make better leaders. As you can see, none of these is a perfect correlation: smarter

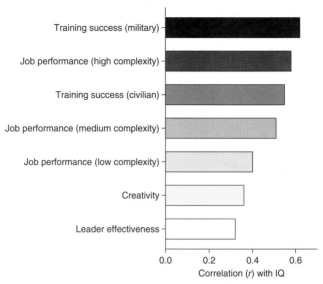

▲ Figure 3.1 Correlation of IQ with different aspects of job performance. (Figure adapted from Kuncel and Hezlett, 2010, with permission from Sage.)

people don't always do better, and there are always other non-intellectual factors that contribute to good performance. But if employers were to select workers using intelligence tests – as many already do – they'd be more likely to get a more productive workforce. There simply isn't another tool that gives such a good *general* prediction of how people will do at work across such a variety of jobs.

Of course, better job performance normally translates to a higher income. Income is one of the most important indicators of social class (or social status), a general concept that can also take into account the type of job you have (sociologists categorize them on a scale from 'manual labour' up to 'professional'), whether you rent or own your home, how many cars you have, the amenities available in your neighbourhood, and more. However you want to measure it – and the best measures of class will take into account many different factors – your score on an intelligence test will correlate with your social class: smarter people tend to end up in higher social classes. As with job performance, the relation of class to IQ is nowhere near as strong as that for education: the correlations are usually in the region of $r = 0.30$ to 0.50 (Strenze, 2007).

Hold on – isn't there a chance we've got this the wrong way around? I've implied that higher IQs lead to higher social class. But don't children who start life in lower social classes tend to have poorer life chances because of their poorer environment? Perhaps, then, the reason IQ tests are predictive of job performance and social class is because they're actually just a measure of the social class someone grew up in. To put it another way, maybe it's not that IQ *causes* better job performance but, instead, higher social class causes both better job performance *and* higher IQ.

This is an argument that's regularly levelled at scientists studying intelligence, and there are a few important points to make in response. First, social class can indeed have important effects on IQ; some of these are discussed in Chapter 5. Also, as we saw for the educational outcomes mentioned above, nobody has ever claimed that intelligence is the only thing that matters in the world of work: numerous other factors make a crucial difference. One other factor that's commonly cited is 'emotional intelligence', discussed in the following box.

Emotional intelligence

The world of work is particularly prone to fads for techniques that claim to improve productivity. The techniques often have very little evidence to back them up. Is the recent trend for measuring 'emotional intelligence' just one of these? Emotional intelligence (sometimes called 'EQ') is presented as a measure of the ability to understand the way that you and others are feeling, which would clearly be of importance in jobs that involve dealing with people. The question is, does EQ tell us any more than the measures psychologists already use, like IQ and personality tests? Several studies have shown that emotional intelligence is linked to better performance at work. Importantly, though, it's not as strongly linked to that performance as IQ (Joseph and Newman, 2010). This may be because we're simply better at measuring IQ. Some researchers argue that EQ is just a trendy, and less useful, re-description of what we already knew.

You might think that social class and intelligence are inextricably intertwined, but researchers have tried to disentangle them by collecting data on large samples of people's 'social mobility' – their movement up and down the social ladder throughout their lives. They might measure the social class a person is born into, their intelligence as a child, then the social class they end up in by the age of, say, 40 (along with a host of other variables). Such studies have been carried out in many Western countries and, in general, they show that the relationship goes both ways: childhood social class has moderate links to intelligence, but intelligence also makes its own prediction of how people will do in life, over and above the class where they started off (Deary, 2005). Studies like these are evidence of at least a partial 'meritocracy': although there are crucial effects of social origins, opportunities and, of course, pure luck, people with higher ability do tend to end up in jobs where their skills can be put to good use.

Again, it's not too much of a stretch to link higher social class to better health: those in higher classes tend to lead less stressful lives and live in less polluted neighbourhoods, with access to better medical facilities. They're also more likely to take better care of themselves. We'll now look in more detail at the health benefits of a higher IQ.

▶ Health and mortality

Brighter people tend to do healthier things: they exercise more, eat better and are less likely to smoke (Gottfredson, 2004). This might be down to their better education, or their greater ability to sensibly interpret the constant buzz of health-related information in the media. We also saw above that higher-IQ people tend to end up in higher social classes. As we've discussed thus far, these all seem very plausible reasons for the IQ–mortality link mentioned at the beginning of the chapter.

Indeed, studies from the relatively new field of cognitive epidemiology (the study of the links between intellectual abilities and health and disease) have repeatedly found correlations between health and intelligence: smarter people are somewhat less likely to have medical conditions, like heart disease, obesity or hypertension, that decrease life expectancy. This is found for mental as well as physical health: large-scale studies have shown that those with lower intelligence test scores are more likely to be hospitalized for psychiatric conditions (Gale et al., 2010). The link seems particularly strong for schizophrenia: there might be a biological connection between schizophrenia and intelligence, and being more intelligent might help patients cope with the disorder's often frightening and confusing symptoms (Kendler et al., 2014). The IQ–health connection is found even controlling for social class, and is even found in very rich countries with free, first-class health care available to all (for example, one study found the link in Luxembourg (Wrulich et al., 2014)).

It's no surprise, then, that there's such an impressive link between intelligence and mortality. Figure 3.2 illustrates this relation with data from a Swedish study of almost a million men. People in the lowest of the nine IQ categories were over three times more likely to die in the 20 years after their testing session than those with the highest IQ scores. As you can see from the graph, moving along to the higher IQ categories is like walking down a staircase: the higher the IQ, the lower the risk of death. A review study, taking into account all the evidence, reported its results in terms of IQ points, rather than categories: they concluded that being 15 IQ points higher in childhood led to a 24-per-cent lower risk of death in the subsequent years (Calvin et al., 2010). As mentioned above, some studies find that the size of the effect of low IQ on mortality risk is similar to that of other more commonly studied risk factors, like smoking.

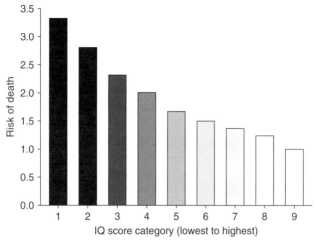

▲ Figure 3.2 IQ and mortality risk. In a sample of nearly one million Swedish men, the risk of death (from any cause) in the 20 years following the IQ test was substantially higher for those with lower IQ scores. If the risk of death for the highest IQ category (group 9) is 1.0, the graph tells us the comparative risk for the other groups. The risk is over three times higher in the lowest IQ category (group 1). (Data from Batty et al., 2008.)

It's always important to look for alternative explanations. There are at least two other ways of thinking about the IQ–death connection (Deary, 2008). The first is that lower intelligence is not a cause, but simply an *indicator* of poorer health. This harks back to the above discussion of social class: maybe being brought up in a poorer social class – perhaps with worse nutrition – lowers intelligence *and* means that you'll be less healthy throughout your life, and this is why it appears that they're linked. Some evidence for this idea comes from studies showing that higher-IQ people tend to have slightly more symmetrical faces (Bates, 2007). Facial symmetry is an indicator of healthier development in the womb and in early life: it might be that developmental problems (like infections or accidents) affect the brain, too, and thereby affect intelligence.

The second alternative is a genetic one: maybe the genes that give some people generally healthier bodies than others – for example, some people have hearts and circulatory systems that are more efficient – also give them healthier brains (this is known as a 'genetic correlation'). That is, some people may be 'better built' than others, and this goes for their brains as well as their other organs. In both of these alternatives, lower IQ is itself the consequence of factors that are themselves the cause of poorer health and earlier death.

The two alternative scenarios are unlikely to be the whole story, because the intelligence–mortality link isn't all down to health and disease. After researchers control for these factors and for social class, the link is smaller, but it's still there. What else might explain it? In one huge study of a million Swedish men, who had their IQs tested upon entry into the military, researchers found that lower IQ meant a greater chance of being murdered in the following few decades (Batty et al., 2008). It's also been shown that lower IQs relate to higher risk of death in accidents. The researchers who found these links have suggested that higher-IQ people are better at noticing and responding to risks, making them less likely to get caught up in life-threatening situations.

As I said at the outset, the connection between intelligence and mortality is complex. All of the factors we've discussed above – education, jobs, social class, health, genetics, risk perception, and more – are likely to play a role in a complicated chain of cause and effect (Figure 3.3 shows one possible model of this chain). But by linking scores from intelligence tests to medical data, cognitive epidemiologists are beginning to unravel the complexity, explaining why being smarter extends your life.

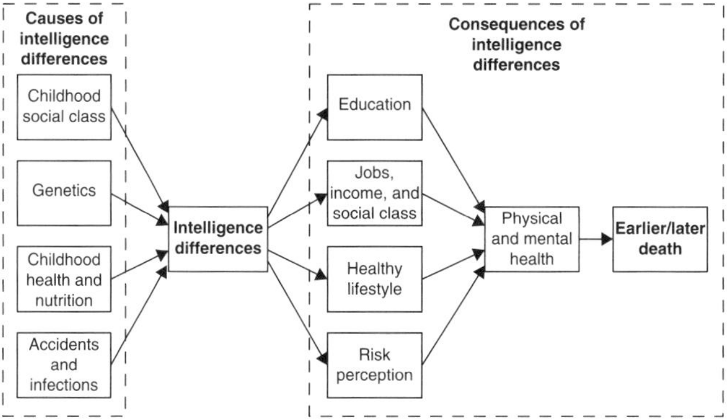

▲ Figure 3.3 A simple model of cognitive epidemiology, connecting the factors discussed in this chapter. Each arrow implies a causal path: for example, better nutrition as a child leads to a higher IQ, which helps in getting a job with higher income, which improves health, thus leading to a later death. In reality, many more variables are involved, and factors such as education and income are influenced by more than just intelligence. (Figure adapted from Batty et al., 2007, with permission from Sage.)

Everything else

Exam grades, job performance, health, mortality: all the topics we've discussed so far make intelligence sound a bit serious and clinical. It helps you lead a longer, healthier life (perhaps like eating a hearty breakfast every morning) but there's a lot more to intelligence than this.

People often argue that IQ tests are measuring a particular kind of 'academic' intelligence, and miss out on the sort of creativity that helps produce art and invent new technologies. The tests do, however, correlate positively (and moderately strongly) with the sorts of measures psychologists use in the lab in an attempt to quantify creativity (such as the 'alternative uses' task, where people have to come up with as many creative uses as they can for, say, a brick; Nusbaum and Silvia, 2011). IQ test scores also associate with the sensory ability to discriminate between musical tones and rhythms, which is crucial for musical creativity (Mosing et al., 2014). Some studies have also suggested that people who score higher on IQ tests also tend to have more patents and artistic prizes (Wai et al., 2005). Of course, much sets true creative geniuses apart from other smart people: personality, persistence and interests, among other qualities, will all play major roles. But we shouldn't ignore the essential role that the *g*-factor plays in creativity.

Another type of creativity that has been studied with regard to IQ is scientific and mathematical creativity: the sort of insight that leads to a 'Eureka!' moment when working on a problem. It seems that higher spatial ability – measured by, among other things, the 'mental rotation' task we encountered in Chapter 2 – seems to be particularly helpful (Wai et al., 2009). The kind of abstract visualization that's required to manipulate shapes in one's mind seems to be essential for thinking through new scientific questions.

Now for an even more controversial topic: it would be quite something if intelligence tests were able to predict what a person thought about lofty issues such as how society should be organized, or the existence of a supreme being in the universe. Surprising as it may seem, IQ tests are indeed related to political and religious beliefs. For example, research shows that higher intelligence scorers tend to be less racist, less sexist, and less accepting of authoritarian parenting and policing: that is, more socially liberal. Even after controlling for social class and education, one study found a correlation of $r = 0.45$ between IQ and social liberalism (Deary et al., 2008). Higher-IQ people are also more interested in politics in general, being more likely to turn out to vote in elections. Left-leaning readers shouldn't feel too smug upon reading this, though: the evidence seems to show that higher-IQ people are *economically* as well as socially liberal, tending to be in favour of freer markets (Carl, 2014).

As if politics wasn't a touchy enough topic, IQ researchers have also studied religion. Around 60 analyses from across the past century have converged on the finding that there's a small correlation between strength of religious belief (measured, for example, by asking people how much they agree that the Bible is the word of God) and intelligence. The correlation is negative, such that smarter people tend to be less religious. The link is pretty weak: a recent meta-analysis estimated it at around $r = 0.25$ (there's a stronger negative link between intelligence and 'fundamentalist' religious beliefs than more liberal, 'spiritual' ones; Zuckerman et al., 2013). Intelligence differences don't explain much of the variation in religiosity, but it is a consistent finding, and it's independent of education level: there does appear to be something about having a higher IQ that makes people less religious.

Finally, given most of what we've discussed thus far, you might wonder whether having a higher IQ makes you happier. After all, those with higher-level jobs, higher incomes and better health tend to report greater levels of life satisfaction. Strangely, for many years the research on this question was equivocal. However, recent studies of larger samples have confirmed that brighter people report higher wellbeing, and that, to a large extent, this is due to the effects of IQ on the kinds of socio-economic and medical factors we've discussed (Ali et al., 2013).

We've now seen some examples of the impressive range of aspects of life that are related to IQ test scores. The remainder of the chapter addresses two further questions: Does IQ stop mattering once you get above a certain score? And are there any negative things that come with having a higher IQ?

▶ How high is high enough?

Only just over 2 per cent of people get scores above 130 on a properly 'normed' IQ test (see Figure 2.2). Are they any better off than people with perfectly respectable and above-average scores of, say, 115 or 120? The psychologists Camilla Benbow, David Lubinski and their collaborators have led a study for decades in an attempt to answer this question. Unlike other studies, which usually try to collect a sample of people that's representative of the general population, their study specifically selected teenagers who performed well above average on the SAT, a test often taken at school in the US that's close in content to an IQ test.

One subset of this Study of Mathematically Precocious Youth – as it's called, although these youths were also precocious in non-mathematical areas – were the best of the best: their SAT scores were the top 0.0001 per cent of the population. And 30 years after they had taken the SAT, these 320 'scary smart' people (to quote the researchers) had achieved an astonishing amount (Kell et al., 2013). They had become high-ranking politicians, CEOs of companies, high-ups in government agencies, distinguished academics, journalists for well-known newspapers, artists and musical directors. They had been awarded patents, grant money and prizes, and had produced plays, novels, and a huge amount of economic value. They had, in other words, made incalculable contributions to society, for everyone's benefit.

Overall, then, it seems that particularly high IQ scores are related to particularly impressive achievements. Moreover, and importantly for our question here, another analysis by Benbow and Lubinski showed that, even *within* the top 1 per cent of SAT scorers, those with higher IQs were doing better: they had higher incomes and were more likely to have obtained advanced degrees (Robertson et al., 2010). There are, it seems, no limits to the benefits of a high IQ: even within the cleverest people, intelligence keeps on mattering.

The contribution to society made by these high-IQ people – the so-called 'smart fraction' of each country's population – has inspired some to argue that these 'gifted' individuals should be sought out using IQ tests and taught separately, so as to encourage and develop their talents. We'll return to the fractious subject of educational selection in Chapter 6.

When is having a high IQ worse?

By now, I hope you're convinced that higher IQ scores are linked to a whole host of positive outcomes (though I suppose you might disagree when it comes to politics and religion). But is having a higher IQ related to anything *negative*? The answer is: not much.

A common stereotype is that of the boffin who might do well on cognitive tests but fails in everyday social situations. Such people do exist: I know plenty of them. But in representative studies there's no clear evidence for a negative relationship between intelligence and social skills: the sizes of the correlations between cognitive abilities and personality traits like extraversion and agreeableness tend to be close to zero (Wolf and Ackerman, 2005; though again, see the box on emotional intelligence above for a discussion of one attempt to link social and cognitive skills).

There is, however, one negative trait that's consistently linked to higher IQ: short-sightedness (Teasdale et al.,

1988). It really does seem that smarter people are more likely to need glasses. Nobody really knows why, but one theory suggests that it's because smarter children read more from a young age, altering the development of their eyes. I suspect, though, that most people would be willing to pay the price of a mild inconvenience like short-sightedness for all the benefits a higher IQ brings.

There is also some suggestive evidence (Gale et al., 2013) that individuals with extremely high intelligence may be more prone to bipolar disorder (formerly known as 'manic depression'). Some have suggested that this might explain the stereotype of the troubled artistic genius, with the 'manic' phases of the disorder leading to creative outbursts. Many more studies would need to be done to confirm this.

▶ Summary

To a certain degree, life is an IQ test. All of the links we've seen above – between intelligence test scores and exam grades, work efficiency, physical and mental health, creativity, political opinions and even mortality – show that having a higher IQ score has real-life consequences, many of them considerable and the vast majority of them positive. As the psychologist Linda Gottfredson has argued, having a higher general intelligence seems to make you more adaptable to an unpredictable, capricious world. You may have heard the assertion that 'IQ tests only tell you how good you are at doing IQ tests'. With any luck, the research I've described here has persuaded you that this couldn't be further from the truth.

Intelligence is an important part of the web of causes and correlations that psychologists, sociologists and medical researchers try to trace. It's not the full explanation for any of the outcomes discussed here: we should always take social and economic factors into account. But just as importantly we shouldn't forget, as many researchers unfortunately do, that cognitive skills should be part of the equation.

As our societies move towards even more complicated technology and computerization in everyday life, the importance of intelligence – the ability, after all, to catch on to new ideas and solve new problems – will only increase. Indeed, some researchers have argued that the link between intelligence and income strengthened in the West across the twentieth century, as manual labour gradually became less important for success and intellectual ability came to the fore (Marks, 2014).

The points discussed in this chapter, showing the benefits of a higher IQ, raise an important question: can we make people smarter? If we could, it might be one way of making them healthier, more efficient and more creative. Chapter 5 is devoted to answering this question. Before we get there, though, we'll look in Chapter 4 at some of the reasons people might have different IQ scores in the first place: the biology of intelligence.

4

The biology of intelligence

*'"It is a question of cubic capacity,"
said he; "a man with so large a
brain must have something in it."'*

Arthur Conan Doyle, 'The Adventure of the Blue Carbuncle'

I assume most of the people reading this book are more intelligent than a sea slug. The interesting question is why. So far, we've mostly been concerned with intelligence differences between people, but our discussion would be incomplete without at least a consideration of why sea slugs (or any non-human animals) and humans, though they have spent just as long evolving, are so vastly different in their mental abilities. We'll then look at the biological differences, in the genes and in the brain, that have been linked to differences in intelligence.

▶ Evolution and intelligence

The very name of our species, *Homo sapiens*, emphasizes the fact that we're highly intelligent (it translates as 'wise man'). We can assume that, to a great extent, this intelligence is an *adaptation*. In order to survive and successfully reproduce in Darwin's 'struggle for life', our ancestors would have had to adapt to particular challenges and pressures found in their environment.

The most obvious evolutionary pressure, experienced by almost all animals, is to avoid predators. There are many ways to do this: animals have evolved to be very small, or very fast, or have developed armour plates for protection. But another way is to evolve complex thinking skills. These mental abilities are flexible: they also help deal with other pressures, like finding food, surviving a harsh environment, and avoiding (or winning) conflicts with rivals. It certainly seems as if a general ability to think is evolutionarily useful: a number of studies have found a g-factor of intelligence in the simple cognitive tests given to species ranging from primates to mice and birds, indicating they've each evolved general cognitive toolkits in their own ways (Bouchard, 2014).

But our abilities are clearly on a different level from those in our non-human cousins. The psychologist Steven Pinker (2010) has suggested that humans have adapted to the 'cognitive niche': just as some animals thrive by living in the tops of trees, or by flying, or by becoming parasites on other animals, our special remit is our high level of intelligence. But how did we evolve thinking abilities that are so much more impressive than those of other animals?

The usual story told about the evolution of human intelligence concerns the increasing size of the brain. A huge number of our ancestors' skulls have been discovered, mainly in Africa, by paleoanthropologists. If you line these skulls up in chronological order, the most obvious thing you'll notice is that they get bigger: the capacity of the skull has increased substantially across time (see Figure 4.1). We can assume that this is because of the expanding brain within it.

There's little reason to doubt that larger brains mean better cognition: more brain cells allow for more complex mental processing, in much the same way as adding more RAM to your computer will allow it to run more software without crashing. The archaeological

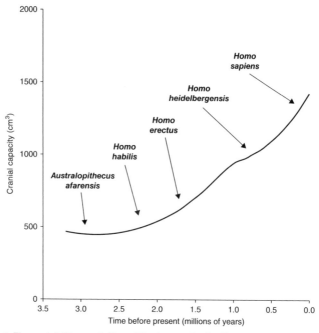

▲ Figure 4.1 The evolution of the human brain. The cranial capacity (skull size) of our ancestors, estimated from the sizes of fossilized skulls, has increased across time. Shown on the graph are the names of different ancestral species, and our species, indicating the approximate time of their first appearance in the fossil record. (Data from Potts, 2011.)

record certainly shows increases in the complexity of tool use, society and culture alongside the growth in brain volume. But the brute size of the brain is far from the full story on the evolution of intelligence. After all, the brains of elephants are much larger than ours, and whereas they're smart compared to most other animals, nobody is predicting that they'll be launching rockets to the moon any time in the near future.

As well as the size, the *complexity* and *organization* of our brains changed across evolutionary time. Think of it like an army: having a very large number of soldiers will help you win battles, but another way to win is to have a smaller army that's equipped with more advanced technology. The smaller army might also be more efficient, using fewer precious resources. This is an important consideration in evolution: large brains consume a lot of energy, and this downside of becoming ever larger may have outweighed the advantages.

We are still in the dark about the details of cognitive and brain evolution. Exactly how and when our brains became larger and more complex remains to be discovered. Future researchers will have to take into account human faculties like language, sociability and culture, which might have acted as virtuous circles: after they themselves evolved, they likely spurred the evolution of ever more complex cognition.

We'll discuss brains in more detail below. For now, consider that natural selection works on differences in our DNA, picking up on genetic mutations that give a fitness or survival advantage. This implies that some genetic differences can be more or less beneficial to our cognitive abilities. Does this mean that genetics might explain why some people today are smarter than others?

▶ Different kinds of genetics

We now enter the realm of 'behavioural genetics'. Importantly, it comes in two flavours. The first asks 'To what extent do genes contribute to intelligence differences?' and is called **quantitative genetics**. The second asks 'Which are the specific genes in the DNA that, when they differ among people, cause intelligence differences?' and is called **molecular genetics**. This is a subtle distinction, and it often causes confusion. The point is this: we can know whether there are genetic effects on intelligence (from quantitative genetics) without knowing any of the specific genes involved (that is, without knowing the molecular genetics).

▶ Are there genetic effects on intelligence?

How can it be possible to know about genetics without looking at DNA? Scientists have addressed this question by studying twins (as with so many things, the twin study was Francis Galton's idea, though he didn't quite work out the method described below). There are, of course, two types of twin. Identical twins, who develop from the same egg, have near-100-per-cent identical DNA – that is, they are clones of one another, give or take a few unique mutations. Fraternal twins develop from different eggs and are as related to each other as are any regular siblings: they share around 50 per cent of their DNA. A vast amount of knowledge in quantitative genetics has been gained from comparing these two types of twin. Here's how.

Take a large sample of twins and give them all an IQ test. Then, split them into identical and fraternal types, and compare the IQ of one twin to that of their co-twin. What you'd find is that the identical twins are much more similar in their IQ scores than are the fraternal twins. The only possible reason for this is genetic: after all, the only thing that differs between the two types of twins that would make them more similar – so long as each pair is raised in the same family – is the percentage of genes they share.

Let's add some numbers. Imagine that the IQ correlation (see Chapter 1) between identical twins is around 0.80 (about the same as the correlation between two sittings of the test by the same person) and that between fraternal twins is lower, at around 0.55. We enter these numbers into the following equation, called 'Falconer's Formula', which is pretty much the '$E = mc^2$' of behaviour genetics:

$$h^2 = 2(r_{identical} - r_{fraternal})$$

I admit that it's not quite as catchy as $E = mc^2$. What it does to work out the 'heritability' (called 'h^2') is simple: it takes the difference between the IQ correlations in identical and fraternal twins ($r_{identical} - r_{fraternal}$), and multiplies it by two, because identical twins are twice as similar genetically as fraternal twins. From the numbers above, we get 2(0.80–0.55), which equals 0.50. To reiterate, there can only be a difference in the correlations because of genetics. Converting the result into a percentage, this tells us that 50 per cent of the differences in intelligence are due to genetic differences. In behavioural genetic terminology, intelligence is 50 per cent 'heritable' (of course, behaviour genetics uses many more complex methods than just this one formula: for the details, see Plomin et al., 2013).

I didn't pick those numbers at random: on average, behaviour genetic studies of intelligence have found this same 50 per cent figure. That is, half of the reasons why people vary on intelligence test scores are genetic. Intriguingly, it's been found that the genetic effect on intelligence is stronger in adults (heritabilities of up to 80 per cent) than it is in children (around 20 per cent), suggesting that our biology becomes more important for our intelligence as we age (Plomin and Deary, 2014). Perhaps different genes come into play as we get older, or the ability of the environment to influence intelligence wanes. Regardless of the age, though, so long as intelligence can reliably be measured, twin studies show that it's substantially heritable.

Twin studies have come in for criticism. For example, some wonder whether the reason identical twins are so similar is actually because people *treat* them more similarly. Parents might, for instance, dress them in matching clothes. These criticisms are rarely thought through (why would being dressed alike affect your intelligence?) and have been addressed at length by twin researchers. But even if they hadn't, there are other, complementary methods of estimating heritability. For example, adoption studies, where we compare the IQs of adoptees with the IQs of their adoptive versus their biological parents, give comparable results to twin studies (Plomin et al., 1997).

Four things heritability *doesn't* tell us

1 Heritability doesn't say that 50 per cent of an *individual person's* intelligence is due to their DNA. The heritability estimate is a group figure, describing the reasons for the variance in intelligence among the sample of people studied.

2 Heritability doesn't tell us anything about the average level of intelligence. Intelligence can be 50 per cent heritable in a group where the average IQ is 85, 100, 115 or any other number.

3 'Heritable' doesn't mean the same thing as 'hereditary'. These words are often confused: a 'hereditary' trait is simply anything that's passed on from parents to offspring, whereas 'heritability' is about the genetic variation in that trait.

4 Heritability isn't unique to intelligence. More or less every human trait that varies between people – including height, personality, political attitude and susceptibility to disease – is heritable (that is, genes explain some of the variation). Even educational achievement is heritable, though studies have found that this is partly because it shares its genetic basis with that of intelligence (Krapohl et al., 2014).

Excitingly, a new technique called 'GCTA' (which stands for Genomewide Complex Trait Analysis, but is also the four 'letters' of the bases of DNA – see what they did there?) allows researchers to calculate heritability directly from the DNA of large groups of people, with no need for twins or adoptees, or the assumptions of those kinds of studies. It asks whether people with similar patterns in their DNA – again, without knowing any of the specific genes – tend to have similar IQ scores. As we'd predict from the twin studies, they do. GCTA estimates of heritability mesh with the twin and adoptee estimates (Davies et al., 2011), and it all hangs together beautifully: genetic differences lead to differences in intelligence.

▶ 'Nurture' – the other side of the coin

If that was the 'nature' part of 'nature vs nurture', what does the 'nurture' part involve? 'Nurture' implies parenting, but non-genetic effects on intelligence are far broader than that. For this reason, even though the phrase 'nature versus nurture' is used regularly, it confuses more than it explains (with apologies to Francis Galton – yes, him again – who coined it). 'Genes vs environment' is better, although 'environment' is still a little vague.

The term 'environment' is vague because in twin studies, 'environment' is split into two types: 'shared' and 'non-shared'. The 'shared' environment covers all the things that might make a pair of twins more similar to each other: parenting style, the number of books in the home, the social class of the neighbourhood, and more. 'Non-shared' environment covers the things that make twins different: particular teachers, peer groups, or just serendipitous experiences that happen to either one of the pair.

What's surprising to many is that, taking into account all the data from twin studies, the shared environment appears to have a very small effect on intelligence. If you measure intelligence in adulthood, almost all of the variance is explained by a combination of genes and the non-shared environment. Outside of cases of abuse or neglect, the things that parents do don't seem to have a strong effect on their children's intelligence, in the long run (Harris, 2009). To put this another way, the main reason smart parents tend to have smart children is because of the genes they pass on, not because of their parenting decisions.

There's an extra complication here, though: heritability might differ depending on the environment (a process called **gene-by-environment interaction**). Indeed, logically, it has to. Imagine we created a society with no 'environmental' variation: every child was raised identically, attended identical schools, had identical friends, and the rest. We'd actually see *higher* heritability, since the only thing left to vary would be the genes. It's been suggested that, in this way, the heritability of intelligence (or any other trait) can be viewed as an indicator of how equal our society is (Asbury and Plomin, 2014). There is evidence that – at least in countries that don't have extensive welfare states and thus tend to have wider disparities in their environments – heritability tends to be higher in the children of families at the higher end of the social class spectrum (Bates and Tucker-Drob,

2014). It might be that underprivileged environments stifle, to some extent, the intellectual potential that lies in a child's genes.

▶ What are the genes for intelligence?

Since genes often have many functions, we shouldn't really ask about genes for intelligence. It makes more sense to ask whether we've yet found any specific genes that are *linked to* intelligence. Perhaps these genes are involved in making the brain more efficient; maybe they increase the number or improve the structure of neurons, or make the person more able to capitalize on environmental inputs like education. Finding these genes will be interesting, not just for understanding the deep biology of intelligence, but also for medical reasons: for example, we might be able to use a genetic test to predict who will suffer most from the old-age cognitive decline discussed in Chapter 2.

So far, we haven't made much progress on the molecular genetics of IQ. For a few decades, genes with intriguing names like *KLOTHO* and *COMT* and *SNAP-25* had been studied, always with plausible theories to link them to intelligence (for instance, *SNAP-25* had previously been linked to the release of learning-related 'neurotransmitter' chemicals). The problem with these 'candidate gene' studies was that they tended to include very small samples of people. Almost invariably, when independent scientists tried to replicate the findings in larger samples, the story fell apart. The genes were not, in fact, related to intelligence: the original studies had been flukes (Chabris et al., 2012).

The researchers had hit a wall, but on the plus side they had learned a fundamental fact about intelligence: it is **polygenic**. This means that, instead of just a few genes each contributing a large amount, many, many genes that often vary between people each have tiny effects on the variation in intelligence. Candidate gene studies were aiming at the wrong kind of target; there is no single gene, or even handful of genes, for intelligence (though see the box below for some exceptions to this rule). Instead, the intelligence-linked genes turn out to be many thousands of tiny needles in the massive haystack of the human genome. Studies of small numbers of people are only sensitive enough to find large effects, so it's not surprising that previous research didn't uncover any solid results.

To hunt down this large number of tiny genetic effects, geneticists have had to move on to the new 'Genome-Wide Association Study' (or GWAS). Here, thousands of participants have their DNA sampled and their intelligence – or whatever other trait is of interest – tested, and the researchers attempt to relate their intelligence scores to the presence of particular genes. These studies often involve groups of researchers from across the world, collaborating to increase the sample size.

Genetics and learning disabilities

It seems that the genes involved in explaining normal differences in intelligence are common variations, numbered in their thousands, each with a small effect on brainpower. But it is possible for some genetic differences to have profound effects on intelligence. These are the large genetic errors (mutations) that can cause learning disabilities by making major disruptions to the normal functioning of cells. Many genetic disorders, like Down Syndrome or Fragile X Syndrome, involve a substantial intellectual impairment, and are often associated with older parental age. Older parents pass on larger numbers of more minor genetic errors, too, and some researchers have suggested that these might cause small decreases in the IQs of their children. There is currently dispute in the scientific literature about the size – and, indeed, the existence – of this effect (Arslan et al., 2014).

Few GWASs of intelligence have been done so far, but a few genetic variants that seem to relate to intelligence have nonetheless been found (Davies et al., 2015). They include a gene called *APOE*. People with one type of the *APOE* gene tend to have lower intelligence in later life, and also have faster mental decline with age (Schiepers et al., 2012). This might be because the gene is involved in building important parts of the structure of neurons. One gene, though, does not get us very far: the genetics of intelligence is very much a work in progress. I feel confident in predicting that, within the next ten years, GWASs will have turned up a large number of intelligence-related genetic variants.

Above, I mentioned the prospect of genetic testing to predict cognitive decline. Once we know a decent number of the genes that contribute to intelligence, the floodgates are open for another kind of test: prenatal screening for intelligence. Would parents who found out that their unborn child had relatively few of the high-IQ-linked genes wish to terminate the pregnancy? The eugenicists we encountered in Chapter 1 would be rubbing their hands at the idea, but would this type of procedure be acceptable in the modern world? Given the rapid advance of GWAS, we need a measured, informed debate over the ethics and legality of prenatal selection for intelligence, and we need it soon: if my prediction is correct, it won't be long before the practice catches up with the theory.

▶ Intelligence and the brain

The genes relating to IQ will, of course, have their effects in the brain. People differ in both the quantity and quality of their brain tissue, and in the past few decades we have been able to measure these aspects using techniques like Magnetic Resonance Imaging (MRI) scans. How clear a picture have these given us of the neuroscience of intelligence?

Think back to the long, slow increase in brain size throughout our evolutionary history (see Figure 4.1). As we learned, as the brain size of our species increased, so too did our capacity for complex thought. It turns out that this applies when comparing modern people, too: those with bigger brains have higher IQs. This finding has been highly controversial, but it is now so well established and well replicated that it's pointless to deny it. Again, it makes sense that having more neurons to think with is advantageous. Indeed, a recent review of 148 studies (Pietschnig, 2014) concluded that the correlation between brain volume and intelligence test scores is relatively small, at $r = 0.24$. Having said that, there is no reason to think that one very broad brain measurement should explain everything (or even a substantial amount) about any psychological trait.

Going beyond brute size and looking at specific brain areas gives us a more nuanced view. Most commonly studied are the frontal lobes, the parts of the brain just above the eyes and directly behind the forehead. Patients with damage to their frontal lobes caused by head injuries, strokes or infections have particular trouble with tests of 'fluid' intelligence (see Chapter 2), which involve abstract thinking. This has led some prominent researchers, like neuroscientist John Duncan (2010), to hypothesize that the frontal lobes are responsible for tasks particularly relevant for intelligence, such as planning, organizing and reasoning.

The frontal lobes are of particular interest right from the beginning of life. We know from one beautiful study (Shaw et al., 2006) that the thickness of the cortex (the 'grey matter' that forms the outer part of the brain) develops differently in high-IQ children than in those of more modest ability, especially in the frontal lobes. Everyone's cortex starts out thickening until the start of adolescence and then begins to thin down, probably because redundant connections are pruned away to improve efficiency. The key finding of the study was that the cortex stayed thicker for longer in the high-IQ children. This extra period of thickness might have allowed more time for complex, useful brain networks to be built, leading to better scores on the tests.

The frontal lobes are connected to other parts of the brain that are also essential for complex thought. In what is the best-supported theoretical model of intelligence and the brain, called the 'P-FIT' (for Parieto-Frontal Integration Theory), neuroscientists Rex Jung and Richard Haier (2007) suggest that intelligence is particularly dependent on a brain network that links the frontal lobes to the parietal lobes. This latter part of the brain (see Figure 4.2) is thought to collect and organize perceptual information (which is processed in yet other areas of the brain), then feed it forward to the frontal lobes, which in turn begin to reason their way through problems.

The P-FIT model emphasizes that the parietal and frontal areas need to send information between one another. To do that, they rely on another kind of brain tissue, the 'white matter'. White matter cells – so-called because of the white-coloured insulation material, myelin, that surrounds their long, tendril-like axons – are grouped together in million-strong bundles known as 'tracts', which connect up, and

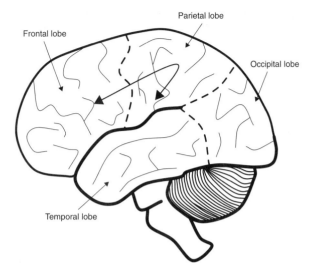

▲ Figure 4.2 Diagram of the human brain, viewed from the left, indicating the different lobes. The double-headed arrow shows the main brain circuit implicated in the P-FIT theory. (Diagram by the author, after Jung and Haier, 2007.)

transmit signals between, important areas of the cortex. See Figure 4.3 for an illustration of the brain's white matter tracts.

People vary in the efficiency of these connections, and neuroscientists have come up with an ingenious way of measuring this variation, called 'Diffusion Tensor' MRI. In this kind of MRI scan, the researchers track the diffusion of water molecules that are moving through the cells. If the molecules have a good deal of movement in one direction, along the length of the tract, the inference is made that the tract is making a good connection, and can efficiently pass on the electrochemical signals

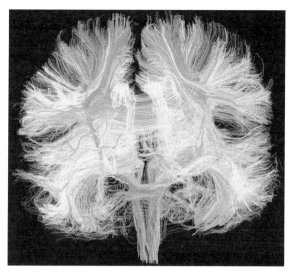

▲ Figure 4.3 The brain's white matter connections seen from the front, viewed using Diffusion Tensor MRI. These connections carry signals throughout the brain, transmitting information between important areas of the cortex. (Image courtesy of Mark Bastin, Centre for Clinical Brain Sciences, The University of Edinburgh.)

that transmit information throughout the brain. If the molecules' movement is more random, this implies that they are often diffusing out of the sides of the tract, and thus some of the signals may be being lost, like in a pipe that has sprung a leak.

Many studies have now shown that this measure of the efficiency of white matter connections is correlated with performance on IQ tests, especially those that involve reasoning and speed. Better connections tend to mean faster and more efficient cognitive abilities (Penke et al., 2012). More evidence for the importance of a well-wired brain comes from the study of the ageing of intelligence. As we get older, the white matter tracts deteriorate, losing their myelin, shrinking in size, and developing scar-like features that may partly block their signals. This deterioration happens alongside the age-related cognitive decline we discussed in Chapter 2, implying that degenerating white matter is among the causes of the loss of thinking skills that happens in later life (Lövdén et al., 2014).

More evidence for the P-FIT model of intelligence comes from *functional* neuroimaging. Everything we've discussed so far comes from *structural* imaging, where the build of the brain and its connections are analysed, but researchers can also ask participants to do IQ tests while they're in the scanner, and study their patterns of brain activity while they do so. One way of doing this is functional MRI, or *f*MRI. As particular brain areas become more active, they require more energy; blood flows to them to provide it, and the *f*MRI scan picks up on the flow. In these studies, the brain areas that 'light up' most commonly on the scans as the IQ tests are completed are – you guessed it – the frontal and parietal regions. Another important finding from functional imaging relates to brain efficiency. Compared to those with lower ability, the brains of higher-IQ people tend to show *less*, rather than more, activity when completing complicated tasks: this suggests that their brains can more efficiently work through the problems.

As with quantitative genetics, multiple complementary lines of evidence converge on the same broad results about the neuroscience of intelligence. It's the frontal and parietal areas of the brain that seem to be most strongly involved in tasks measuring *g*. This isn't to say that the other parts of the brain aren't involved: it's likely that all parts are engaged to some extent (the urban myth that 'we use only 10 per cent of our brain' is just that: a myth). Indeed, Jung and Haier noted areas in both the temporal and occipital lobes (see Figure 4.2) that are regularly found to be active during intelligence testing. But the general finding of most research is that the frontal and parietal brain areas comprise the main circuits that underlie our intellectual abilities. The efficiency with which messages can pass between them might be the foundation of intelligence differences.

▶ Summary

What a time it is to be an intelligence researcher (and not a sea slug). Not only have new DNA-based techniques confirmed the validity of the twin study and reinforced our knowledge about the heritability of IQ, but some of the specific genes that contribute to IQ are just beginning to be found. After decades of purely behavioural measurements, MRI techniques allow us to peer inside the skull and begin to understand how the clump of cells within it can produce complex, intelligent behaviour. The 'holy grail' of this type of research would be a set of studies finding a daisy chain of results: specific genes leading to specific brain differences, which themselves lead to differences in intelligence. We're getting closer all the time.

A common mistake is to come away with the impression that, since intelligence is related to biology, it must be immutable. Nothing in the genetic studies (which never show 100-per-cent heritability) or the neuroimaging (which shows only neural *correlates* of intelligence) leads to that conclusion. Certainly, the genetic results imply that attempts to *equalize* outcomes in areas like education are fool's errands: it will be extremely difficult to eradicate genetically influenced differences between children. There may be biological limits on what we can expect from some people: although intelligence is not immutable, it is unlikely to be infinitely malleable. Even so, there is no reason to be fatalistic, as we will see in the next chapter, which discusses the ways in which we might be able to improve intelligence.

The easy way to raise your IQ

'For use almost can change the stamp of nature...'

William Shakespeare, Hamlet

I admit it: I chose the title of this chapter just to get your attention. You won't find tips on how to become smarter just by reading this, although I hope you will improve your knowledge about intelligence. Hooks like this title are all over the media and the Internet, with eye-catching, click-baiting claims about new techniques, diets, books and video games that apparently have IQ-raising potential. Considering the evidence we saw in Chapter 3, linking higher IQs to better performance in so many spheres, it's no surprise that people are interested in ways to make themselves smarter. Are any of the IQ-boosting claims worth taking seriously?

Before we start, how much would we need to raise IQ for it to be worth while? Happily, it turns out that the answer is 'not very much'. Obviously, it would be wonderful if, with some new training programme or technique, we could take people of average intellect and turn them into geniuses, but, let's face it, this is unlikely. Let's stick with something more achievable: imagine we had a way to raise the IQ of everyone in a country by 5 points. What effect would this have? Think back to Chapter 3, where we discussed the relationship between intelligence and mortality. If a person with an IQ of 100 has a 0.004-per-cent lifetime chance of being killed in a traffic accident (the correct number for the UK, by the way), that chance will be ever so slightly lower in a person with an IQ of 105: perhaps 0.003 per cent, perhaps because of improved risk perception. On an individual level, this won't make much difference. But aggregated across a population of millions, this will mean many fewer deaths (and injuries) from car crashes. With even a small IQ increase, we'd see the overall number of accidents dropping substantially.

The same argument can be made for workplace efficiency: those with slightly higher IQs should, on average, be slightly more productive, and these small effects would add up to rather a lot across the whole country, saving employers a great deal of money as the employees make fewer mistakes and finish more tasks. Small effects can matter a great deal if they're across populations. By raising everyone's IQ by a small amount – so long as the rise was truly an improvement in intelligence and not just in the ability to take a specific test (we wouldn't get very far just by telling people the answers to vocabulary test questions, for instance!) – a country could save enormous amounts.

▶ The 'Mozart Effect'

With that reassuring calculation behind us, we can now discuss some attempts people have made to boost IQ. The first is the 'Mozart Effect'. Some years ago, a paper published in the top science journal *Nature* (Rauscher et al., 1993) reported an experiment where university students were asked to complete several IQ-type tests while either listening to a piece of music by Mozart (for Mozart fans, the piece was the Sonata for Two Pianos in D Major, K448), doing a relaxation technique, or sitting in silence. The results showed that, for spatial IQ tasks only, the students' results were 8 or 9 points higher when listening to Mozart.

The first question you might ask is: 'How on earth can listening to Mozart improve spatial performance in an IQ test?' The original authors vaguely suggested that it was something about the 'complexity' of Mozart's music that facilitated performance. Of course, we don't need to know the mechanism of an effect if it turns out to be robust and reliable.

Sadly, the 'Mozart Effect' is neither robust nor reliable: the original finding was likely a fluke. Many other independent researchers have attempted to replicate the effect, and they have usually found no effect of Mozart at all. In 2010 scientists collected together all the data on the Mozart Effect, and the unusually frank title of their paper nicely sums up their opinion: 'Mozart Effect – Schmozart Effect'. They concluded that, overall, there was no good evidence for Mozart's power to improve intelligence (Pietschnig et al.).

The poor evidence for the Mozart Effect hasn't stopped the development of a huge industry that sells CDs and MP3s of Mozart (and other composers), with the express purpose of boosting IQ (just search your favourite music-purchasing website for 'Mozart IQ' and you'll see dozens of examples). It's almost as if the clocks stopped in 1993, and none of the failed replications of the Mozart Effect ever happened. Even worse, many of the Mozart-IQ CDs are aimed at parents with babies ('Boost your child's IQ with Mozart!'), even though the participants in the original study, and in most of the subsequent ones, were university students. The conclusion is clear: listen to music for its own sake, not because you think it might make you smarter.

▶ Brain training

In the past ten years, a raft of video games has appeared on the market that claim to improve your brain function. They often include simple tasks, such as counting the number of syllables in phrases, to provide seemingly important – but non-scientific – information like your 'brain age'. The vast majority of these games are not based on scientific evidence. But one particular variety of brain training has been extensively studied in the lab. The science behind it turned out to be extremely controversial.

In 2008 it seemed as if our prayers had been answered: there was a simple way to raise intelligence. It was known as the '*n*-back'. The *n*-back task is a simple computer game that trains the 'working memory' skill (see Chapter 2). You are shown a series of letters on the screen, one by one. All you have to do is press a button if the letter you're seeing currently was the same as the letter that appeared *n* letters back in the sequence. It's easy if *n* stands for, say, 2: remembering two letters back doesn't strain your working memory too much. But what if *n* stood for 5, or 7? As you get better at the lower numbers, the computer adapts the task so that it gets more and more difficult.

Take a second to imagine what you'd have to do to perform this task: you'd have to hold every letter in the sequence in memory, constantly comparing them to the new ones that appear and asking yourself 'Is this one the same as five letters ago?' Now imagine doing this task on the computer screen, while *at the same time* doing another, auditory *n*-back task on headphones.

This rather devilish 'dual *n*-back' task was what the hapless participants in the 2008 study were trained on. They did the task for around 30 minutes each day across several weeks. At the end of the study, the authors claimed that not only had the participants improved at the *n*-back task, but the working memory training had 'transferred' to an improvement on a completely different kind of intelligence test, one similar to the 'matrix reasoning' tasks we saw in Figure 2.1 (Jaeggi et al., 2008). It was as if, to return to our gym metaphor from Chapter 3, building up the participants' arm muscles had somehow improved their lung function. This was big news. Had the authors discovered the basic cognitive process that, if trained hard enough, would improve general ability?

I hate to burst such a promising bubble, but the 2008 *n*-back study was a lesson in how *not* to do IQ research. Critics of the paper noted that the authors didn't use the IQ tests properly, failing to use the standard time limits. They also didn't include an 'active' control group – the control participants in the experiment did no activities at all, so even if the *n*-back training caused improvements, we can't be sure that any computer game wouldn't have had the same effect.

Nevertheless, one bad study isn't enough to completely discredit an idea: as with the 'Mozart Effect', other scientists have tried to recreate the *n*-back effect in their own labs (the original researchers have also taken the criticisms on board and performed better-controlled studies). It's fair to say that there have been mixed results. One recent review of the evidence concluded that, overall, there was no evidence that working memory training helped improve general cognitive abilities (Melby-Lervåg and Hulme, 2013). But another suggested that, for older people, the results look more encouraging (Karbach and Verhaeghen, 2014). These contradictions and controversies are the sign of a young scientific field. Research continues apace, and only with larger, longer studies will we find out whether these games really do raise IQ.

'IQ-raising' techniques: questions to ask

1 Is the claim too good to be true? Does it promise a huge IQ increase? If it does, it's very unlikely to be real.

2 Is the claim based on peer-reviewed studies? If someone has data backing up their IQ-boosting claim, it will need to have appeared in a legitimate scientific journal. Anyone can make a claim, but getting it published involves running the gauntlet of peer review, where other scientists will check over your study and ensure that it has no overt flaws. This isn't sufficient to ensure quality, but it is normally necessary to be taken seriously in science.

3 Has the technique been shown to work by anyone except the original proponents? Independent replication is the cornerstone of science. If separate teams of scientists can't make the effect work using the exact same materials under the exact same conditions, it might not be real.

4 Is the effect generalizable? It's no use doing an experiment on students and then claiming that the effect will also appear in babies. The same goes for studies of young adults that are clumsily applied to older people.

▶ Health

We already know that higher-IQ people tend to be healthier. In Chapter 3 we looked at this from a 'cognitive epidemiology' perspective: smarter people make better decisions, making them healthier. But it can also work the other way around: improving health can improve IQ.

To take one example, there is some evidence from developing countries that removing parasitic worms leads to IQ increases in children (Ezeamama et al., 2012). This is perhaps because their systems are no longer disturbed by fighting the parasite, and can devote more resources to brain development. Health effects are also found in more developed countries without severe parasite problems. For instance, there is evidence that after scientists became aware of the toxic effects of lead, and governments banned it from petrol (and thus petrol fumes), children's IQ scores improved as a result (Huang et al., 2012).

Similarly, improving the diet of children who are malnourished has also been shown to improve cognitive abilities. For instance, supplementation with iodine has substantial effects on the intelligence of children who aren't getting enough of it in their diet from milk and seafood (Qian et al., 2005). But we should be careful: this result does not necessarily mean that giving extra dietary supplements to *healthy* children will improve their intelligence. Indeed, the results of experiments on the IQ-boosting propensity of supplements like omega-3 fish oils for healthy children have to date been disappointing (Kennedy et al., 2009).

From supplements, to drugs: researchers are beginning to study synthetic chemicals that might improve cognitive abilities. An improved understanding of the biology of intelligence, as we discussed in Chapter 4, will bring with it more biochemical 'targets' for drugs. As with the genetic issues we also discussed there, the looming appearance on the market of these so-called 'nootropics' means that we need to start having a debate now over the ethics of their use. Few would have problems with nootropic drugs developed to help older people experiencing cognitive decline or even Alzheimer's disease. However, as with 'doping' controversies in sport, will readily available 'smart drugs' mean that students need to take a drug test before sitting an exam? Will richer people gain even more of an advantage in life, since they're more likely to be able to afford the pills? We may not have too long to wait until these become live issues (Cakic, 2009).

▶ Breastfeeding and intelligence

It's often claimed, both in the media and the scientific literature, that a child's intelligence can be improved by breastfeeding. Some long-term studies have found that those who were breastfed as infants have, on average, higher IQs later in life compared to those who were bottle-fed (Mortensen et al., 2002). Does this mean that the nutrients in breast milk, among their many health benefits, help improve intelligence?

Unfortunately, it's not so simple. We know from Chapter 4 that intelligence is partly influenced by genetics, and that the reason higher-IQ parents tend to have higher-IQ children is largely due to genes. What if it's just the case that smarter mothers are more likely to breastfeed (perhaps because they read more about the potential benefits), and the studies are mistaking the transmission of high-IQ genes for an effect of breastfeeding on IQ? Indeed, studies have shown that maternal intelligence is positively related to the likelihood of breastfeeding (Der et al., 2006). A recent review of all the breastfeeding–IQ studies showed that those that controlled for parental IQ or controlled for genetics (by comparing siblings or twins) tended to find much smaller effects, if they found anything at all (Walfisch et al., 2013). The supposed link between breastfeeding and IQ might just be an example of confusing correlation with causation.

The controversy over breastfeeding and intelligence highlights the importance of knowing about genetics. All sorts of claims are made about what parents can do to raise their child's IQ: having books in the home, reading those books to their child, using complex vocabulary in conversation, et cetera. The problem is that all these things tend to be done by cleverer parents, who have already passed on the genes that will make their child more intelligent. Most studies that find a link can't tell whether the parenting or the genetics caused the higher

IQ. This is not to say that these parenting activities definitely don't have any effect on intelligence: it's just that we can only figure out whether they do if we take genetics into account.

▶ Intelligence and education (again)

Earlier, we discussed the fantastical idea that a country might raise the IQ of its entire population. Would it surprise you if I told you that governments have already been doing this for generations? No, they aren't spiking drinking water with experimental chemicals, or broadcasting subliminal Mozart into people's homes while they're asleep. They have, however, been forcing children to do the one thing out of all the methods discussed in this chapter that's most likely to raise IQ: go to school.

We know from Chapter 3 that people who stay in school for longer tend to have higher intelligence test scores. In that chapter, we looked at how being smarter early in life was predictive of staying in school for longer. But the causal arrow might point in both directions: education might also raise people's intelligence test scores. How do we test this idea? It's not as though we can do a randomized experiment, where we randomly select children and ban them from school, comparing their outcomes to those who get an education – their parents might view this as somewhat unethical (though the children themselves may not mind). We have to wait, then, until a 'natural experiment' comes along. As luck would have it, one came along recently.

In the 1960s, the Norwegian government decided to add two extra years of schooling to the mandatory curriculum for all pupils. Two additional pieces of good luck allowed researchers, who came on the scene much later, to turn this into a test of the effects of schooling on IQ. First, the reform was implemented across the different parts of Norway in a staggered way – it happened in some areas years before it happened in others. Second, every male Norwegian sits an IQ test as part of their compulsory army service. In 2012 the researchers were able to compare the later IQ scores of those who had been forced to stay in school for extra years with the scores of those who hadn't (Brinch and Galloway, 2012). They worked out that the extra schooling added 3.7 IQ points per year. This confirmed the results of many other, previous studies that hadn't used such elegant methods.

What's happening in school that might cause these improvements? It isn't clear just yet, and nor do we know exactly which parts of education are the most effective at raising intelligence. One possibility is that the sorts of things learned in school, like arithmetic, general knowledge and reading, might be an effective form of training in the abstract thinking that's required to do well on IQ tests. Maybe staying in school teaches concentration and other skills that help children stay on task, and thus get better IQ test scores. Perhaps the atmosphere of a school improves a child's motivation to do well under testing conditions. Whatever the answer, it's important we find out.

Until now, I've talked about standard schooling: the kind that every child gets as a matter of course. But there have also been intensive educational projects aimed at intervening early to boost the life chances of very disadvantaged children. The two most famous examples are the 'Perry Preschool Project', from the 1960s, and the 'Abecedarian Project' from the 1970s (though there have been many others). In both of these US projects, children deemed to be 'at risk' because of their low social-class backgrounds were given a structured programme of extra preschool teaching to get them prepared for starting education. Because the interventions were done decades ago, we're now able to look at the long-term effects, if any, of the programmes. Whereas a short-term boost to IQ was seen, this tended to peter out by the time the children reached adulthood. By that point, there was hardly any IQ difference between those who got the extra preschool and those who didn't (Barnett, 1998). However, even if IQ wasn't lastingly affected, there did appear to be other extremely valuable effects, such as reduced rates of criminal offending in the preschool group.

Much larger-scale (but, by economic necessity, less intensive) versions of the projects have been run by successive governments in the US and the UK (called Head Start and Sure Start, respectively). There is intense debate over whether the benefits of these interventions are worth the costs (Puma et al., 2010). Even if the efforts until now have been patchy – especially with respect to long-term effects on IQ – they still provide a great deal of useful data. This helps researchers work out the precise ingredients that might help teachers boost children's thinking skills.

▶ The Flynn Effect

Just a moment: it seems that longer schooling, as well as factors like improved nutrition, are beneficial for intelligence. We also know that, for the last century or so, educational opportunities and diets have been improving generation upon generation, at least in the Western world, for almost everyone. Given these points, shouldn't people be brighter now than they were, say, at the start of the twentieth century, just as the average person now is taller than their great-grandparents? In fact, this is exactly what the evidence shows. Intelligence-test performance has been getting better by around 3 points per decade since IQ testing began, in a phenomenon known as the 'Flynn Effect'. It's named after the political scientist James Flynn, who has written about it most extensively.

As we saw in Chapter 2, we define 'average intelligence' as a score of 100 on an IQ test. But during the twentieth century, test-makers started noticing that samples of people born later tended to get average scores of above 100: they were smarter than the 'norm' of the previous generation. As a consequence, tests now have to be continually 're-normed', with their score of 100 being set to the average of a sample of contemporary people.

Why the Flynn Effect matters

It's fascinating for scientists to contemplate the causes of the continual rise in IQ test scores. But, for some, the Flynn Effect is literally a matter of life and death. Those states of the US that still carry out the death penalty are prohibited from executing any criminal who has been diagnosed as intellectually disabled. Recall from Chapter 2 that the (arbitrary) cut-off for disability is an IQ of 70. You'd be ill advised to take a single number from a single IQ test to make such an important decision. But, worse, imagine someone gets a score of just above 70 on a test that was 'normed' a few decades before they took it. The bell curve will have marched upwards since the norming, and the convict's score would be several points lower if the Flynn Effect were taken into account. Without this correction, the person would be executed even though, in reality, they were likely disabled. This issue has occurred several times across the states, such that, in 2014, the US Supreme Court ruled a rigid cut-off score of 70 unconstitutional.

Two questions arise immediately. First, the average person nowadays is hardly a genius, so if we have slowly been gaining IQ points for 100 years, does this mean the average person was intellectually disabled at the beginning of the twentieth century? Second, can increases in factors like education and nutrition explain such a huge (or, to use Flynn's own word, 'massive') increase in intelligence? We know that these factors will add a few IQ points, but can they really account for 30 IQ points across the century?

Flynn, along with other IQ researchers, thinks the answer is no to both these questions. He argues that improved nutrition and education are only part of the explanation of his eponymous effect: a more important reason is because the way we think, as a society, has undergone a revolution across the past 100 years. Flynn recounts the story of the Russian psychologist Alexander Luria, who worked across the late nineteenth and early twentieth centuries. He tested Russian peasants with the 'Similarities' test that we saw in Chapter 2. What, he asked them, do a horse and a dog have in common? A regular answer from the nineteenth-century peasants was: 'They are both used in hunting.' I suspect this isn't the answer that first occurred to you: you will probably have thought of the answer 'They are both mammals.' This illustrates, according to Flynn (2012), the gulf that has opened up between the thinking style of the past and that of the present. Then, the average person thought in concrete ways, focusing on real-world applications and things they had personally experienced. Now, however, people think in a more abstract, 'scientific' manner – we tend to classify the animals as a taxonomist would, and focus on the biological aspects they have in common, rather than thinking of them only in terms of the activity we perform with them. In Flynn's memorable phrase, we all now wear 'scientific spectacles'.

So, at least in Flynn's conception, the average person in the past just wasn't accustomed to the abstract thinking we do so effortlessly in our modern, Western mindset. Computers are everywhere in homes and workplaces, children are explicitly taught science and problem solving in school, and life in general – to borrow a theme from Chapter 3 – has become more like an IQ test. Add this shift in thinking style to improved health, nutrition and education, and we begin to explain the long-term rise in IQ, although we might still need to look at some other factors to fully understand it.

Interestingly, not every one of our mental abilities is increasing. Australian researchers visited a school in 1981 and gave a group of children aged 6–13 two IQ subtests: a test of their processing speed and a test of vocabulary (Nettelbeck and Wilson, 2004). Twenty years later, they returned to the same school, and gave another group of children, also aged 6–13 years, the exact same tests. They were thus able to test whether these two abilities had changed from one generation to another. In line with the Flynn Effect, they found that vocabulary scores had increased: the children in 2001 were better at the test than the children in 1981. But on the speed test there was no generational difference whatsoever. The Flynn Effect – or at least, the Flynn Effect that was operating in Australia between 1981 and 2001 – provided a boost to important skills, but not to how quickly the children's brains could process information. We might see this as good evidence for Flynn's 'cultural' view of the IQ rise: we're getting better at the complex skills that might be more educationally relevant (like knowing words), but not other skills. However, Flynn Effects at different times and in different places might have other causes.

While we're on the subject of the Flynn Effect in different places, one recent review study compared intelligence increases in the developed versus the developing world (Wongupparaj, 2015). What they found is shown in Figure 5.1. Scores have increased everywhere, but they've improved more rapidly in the developing versus the developed world. As the developing world has industrialized, improved the health of its people, and generally become more similar to the developed world,

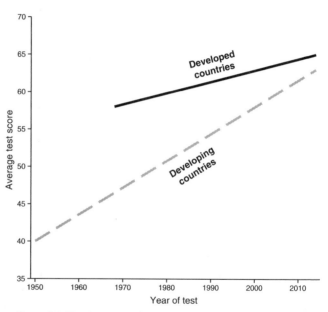

▲ Figure 5.1 The Flynn Effect. Results of a worldwide review of 734 studies that used the Raven's Progressive Matrices test (similar to the 'matrix reasoning' puzzles in Figure 2.1). Intelligence test scores have improved more in the developing world (dashed line) than in the developed world (solid line). Note that the test studied here isn't a full IQ test, so the average score isn't 100. (Figure adapted from Wongupparaj et al., 2015.)

its intelligence test scores have begun to converge with those of the West.

Here's one last question about the Flynn Effect. In the Western, developed world, all children go to school compulsorily. Malnutrition is rare. General health levels are high. Does this mean that the developed world has reached the summit of its intellectual progression, and the Flynn Effect will begin to slow down? Should we expect to see the lines in graphs like Figure 5.1 levelling off as countries get to a certain high point in their development? A review of research in 2014 looked at this very question and concluded that, overall, there is no clear evidence that the effect is stopping, even in very rich countries like the US (Trahan et al., 2014). Whatever it is that's pushing up IQ scores – be it computer use, improvements to education, a cleaner environment, or something we haven't thought of yet – it seems it's still having an effect.

▶ Summary

From a rather depressing start, with the failure of the Mozart Effect and the shaky evidence for the benefits of brain training, we've come to a somewhat more optimistic conclusion. It's difficult for an IQ researcher to be very enthusiastic about new techniques that purport to raise intelligence, after all the disappointments of the past. Certainly, the next time you see a technique, game, supplement or pill that claims to boost your brainpower, regard it with extreme scepticism. Nevertheless, we're lucky that the tools for raising intelligence – which might partly have caused the Flynn Effect – seem to be staring us in the face, in the form of education. Now, intelligence researchers have to find out exactly how education has these effects, and how we can make the most of them.

The glimmers of hope for our ability to raise intelligence might also help put to bed one of the most consistent misunderstandings of intelligence: that IQ is immutable. We'll discuss these criticisms in more detail in the next chapter.

6

Why is intelligence so controversial?

'For if all things were equally in all men, nothing would be prized.'

Thomas Hobbes, Leviathan

The jury is in. The scientific evidence shows that general intelligence can be measured, that it matters in life, that its variation is related to differences in our brains and in our genes, and that we should be at least optimistic that it can be improved. And yet, as I noted in Chapter 1, the idea of intelligence testing is still deeply controversial. Many intelligence researchers shy away completely from even using the word 'intelligence', replacing it with more neutral, euphemistic terms like 'cognitive function' or 'general mental ability'. Why?

In this final chapter, I'll sketch out some of the reasons for the controversy, ranging from a justifiable abhorrence at some of the historical misuses of IQ testing, to political beliefs of all stripes that intrude on what should be objective science. I'll argue that none of these is a respectable reason to ignore or deny the evidence about intelligence that we've seen throughout this book. We'll end with three good reasons to study intelligence.

▌ A tarnished history

As we saw in Chapter 1, many of the originators and developers of intelligence tests were supporters of eugenics. We are absolutely right to find repugnant some of the uses to which intelligence testing was put. Indeed, some of the early researchers, like Galton, would likely have been appalled to see the end results of the eugenics movement. Importantly, though, the immoral beliefs of some of the original scientists are not a reason to dismiss all of their results, many of which, like the existence of the *g*-factor, are well supported by subsequent research. The fact that, for example, the link between smoking and lung cancer was first discovered by Nazi doctors (Proctor, 2000) doesn't mean we should tell people that smoking is healthy after all. Also, it should be remembered that not all of the history of intelligence testing is tainted by eugenics: recall that the first tests were designed by Binet in order to help, not eliminate, children with extra difficulties in education.

At least in theory, the idea of using tests to find the appropriate level of education for everyone was also a virtuous one. But the use of IQ tests in educational selection has created a great deal of animus in the UK: many people place the blame for their bad experiences in school squarely on the '11-plus' selection test (see Chapter 1), and they're often right to do so. The debate on the UK's selective system is not necessarily focused on those children who attended the grammar schools: the evidence seems to show that, as Burt and Thomson envisaged, children from lower social classes did receive an enhancement to their social mobility after getting into a grammar school (Boliver and Swift, 2011). The issue is the dreadful lack of provision for children who didn't pass the test. Many secondary modern schools were notoriously ghastly and had a detrimental effect on the social mobility of children who attended them.

But, again, none of this is an argument against intelligence or IQ. The fact that the British government failed to provide for children in non-grammar schools (which was directly contrary to the wish of Thomson, quoted in Chapter 1) says nothing about the ability of IQ tests to predict which students will go on to do better in life (it might, though, in a world of restricted resources, say something about selective education more generally). The 11-plus exam was an attempt to even out an educational system that, pre-1944, was based to a large degree on the contacts and financial resources of a child's parents, and allow each child to get the appropriate kind of education for their cognitive level (Mackintosh, 2011). It is illogical to blame intelligence testing for the poor implementation of what was an honourable goal.

▶ The desire for equality

Ironically, the desire for true equality of opportunity that was so vociferously expressed by Thomson and Burt is what drives a huge amount of the opposition to IQ tests today. What intelligence research (and differential psychology more generally) tells us is that people's minds are different from one another in measurable ways, that these differences are important in their lives, and that they might be influenced in part by biology. These seemingly obvious facts are unpalatable to many, and have led not only to interminable debates but also to the popularity of evidence-free but comforting alternative views, like the idea of multiple intelligences (see Chapter 2). Two of the most contentious equality battlegrounds in intelligence research are about sex and race differences.

▶ Sex differences in intelligence

Are Martians cleverer than Venusians? The media love any excuse to talk about how there might be sex differences in any psychological trait (laziness, tidiness, fidelity...) but, most of all, they love to talk about whether men are smarter than women, or vice versa. The problem with much of the research on sex differences is that it doesn't have great data. It's extremely rare for researchers to collect intelligence test data on samples that are fully representative of males and females in a country (some of the biggest IQ test samples, as we've seen, are from military service examinations, and these normally include only men). The one country that has tested its entire nation's intelligence is Scotland – it did so in 1932 and again in 1947 as part of the Scottish Mental Surveys. Every 11-year-old in the country was tested on the same IQ test: both samples included well over 70,000 people. The data were recently rediscovered and analysed with reference to sex differences (Johnson et al., 2008). The result, in both samples, was that the average IQ score of girls and boys was exactly the same.

But it's not quite so simple. Just looking at the average hides two consistent sex differences. The first is that there are differences in more specific abilities: women tend to do better than men on verbal measures, and men tend to outperform women on tests of spatial ability (Miller and Halpern, 2014); these small differences balance out so that the average general score is the same. The second is that there is a difference in *variability*: males tend to be over-represented at the very high and the very low levels of intelligence. This was found most clearly in the Scottish data.

There's no consensus on the causes of these differences. Could genetic influences be the root cause of the higher male variability? Are there social or cultural reasons that males might develop a spatial advantage and females a verbal one? Do these explanations make sense, given that the advantage is seen very early in life? It will take a great deal more research to resolve these thorny issues.

▶ Race differences in intelligence

By far the most taboo topic surrounding intelligence, the 'race-IQ controversy' flares up every so often and leads to furious debate. One infamous instance was in 1969, when Arthur Jensen wrote a book-length paper contending that educational and intellectual differences between Black and White Americans were partly due to genetics, and that education had failed to equalize them. Another was in 1994, when Richard Herrnstein and Charles Murray published *The Bell Curve*, a long and detailed book that discussed the importance of intelligence for society, but also argued that different ethnic groups may see different levels of success dependent on their group's average intelligence. The argument extends across countries: some researchers have attempted to collate the results of intelligence tests to show that people in some parts of the world (such as East Asia) are more intelligent than others (such as Europe and Africa).

As you might expect, there is intense disagreement over this kind of research (Nisbett, 2010). Can we be so sure, ask some researchers, that any *IQ* differences between races really reflect *intelligence* differences (that is, are the tests culturally biased against some groups)? And even if we could be, how certain are we that differences are genetic, and not caused by social or economic differences (such as historical or current poverty and racism)? Genes influence intelligence, but this doesn't necessarily mean that they influence group differences in intelligence, too. Also, if there are country-level differences in intelligence, shouldn't we expect them to narrow over time, as poorer countries develop and experience their own Flynn Effects (see Chapter 5)? The answer to all these questions is, unfortunately, that we don't really know. The area is so toxic and scandal-prone that most researchers (and research funders) give it a wide berth. This means that there's far less high-quality research in this area than in the other topics we've discussed (see Hunt and Carlson, 2007, for a good summary of the issues).

▶ Is IQ immutable?

The greatest discomfort occurs when genetics is mentioned. If genes are responsible for differences in IQ, doesn't this mean that IQ is immutable, set in stone from birth? And if that's true, is the desire for a more equal society a forlorn hope? These fears aren't just voiced by people on the left of the political spectrum: to some on the right, the idea of genetic influences on intelligence threatens their belief that hard work and elbow grease are what set successful people apart.

A simple misunderstanding is at the root of these worries. As we saw in Chapter 4, genes don't explain 100 per cent of IQ differences, and the environment has a substantial role. Moreover, as we saw in Chapter 5, there is nothing in principle to stop us from improving intelligence, at least to a degree. We should take the flashy claims of 'brain training' game developers with a large pinch (or perhaps an entire mine) of salt, but there are a number of promising leads that might mean that, in future, we can enhance people's thinking skills. Indeed, there's compelling evidence that IQs have already been rising across the twentieth century and into the twenty-first, as part of the Flynn Effect. And we know that a host of other factors besides intelligence, like personality, effort, motivation and a bit of luck, are vital for a successful life.

We should take a step back and wonder whether it's realistic to wish that everyone had exactly the same degree of mental ability. We don't seem to have a similar desire to equalize, for instance, sports performance: we know that people differ wildly in their athletic abilities, from Olympians at one end of the spectrum to wheezy desk-jockeys like me at the other. Nobody is offended by these differences: indeed, we're very happy for people with exceptional sporting ability, and go to great lengths to support them. Instead of railing against cognitive inequalities, which will likely be very difficult to shift, it may be more productive to make efforts to raise the intelligence of everyone across the board, whether they're low or high to begin with.

A thought experiment

The psychologist Steven Pinker takes this argument a step further in his book *The Blank Slate* (2002). Consider an imaginary world where intelligence is completely determined by the environment, and there's no biological influence whatsoever. There's no reason, Pinker argues, to think this would be a better place: every single child born into a poor family would be forever limited by their background, and an unscrupulous government could easily use social policy to shape, control and hold down its people. Indeed, this kind of social engineering was attempted by several communist regimes in the twentieth century who held 'blank slate' beliefs about human nature. Those who deny the biological aspect of intelligence for moral or political reasons should be careful what they wish for.

There's a more general problem with moral and political objections to scientific findings, which has been described by the philosopher Peter Singer (1995). If your belief in equal rights and opportunities for all – and against racism, sexism and other kinds of discrimination – is based on there being no biological differences between people, then you'll find it very hard to know what to do if clear evidence of biological differences actually appears. If a hundred scientific papers were published tomorrow providing bulletproof evidence that women had higher general intelligence than men, or vice versa, would this justify sexism? Of course not. It makes better sense to base one's moral beliefs on ethical principles that are informed by, but not shackled to, the vagaries of the scientific evidence. One of these principles might be equality of opportunity, regardless of biological make-up or social background.

▶ The IQ debate

As if worries around equality and immutability were not enough, controversy has been stoked by a slew of books and articles that are hostile to the idea of intelligence testing. Some of this criticism is made easier because of the nature of IQ research. Since the questions asked are often about people's lives, they can't be answered under the strictly controlled experimental conditions that are used in other branches of science, like chemistry or physics. And since the questions are so complex, the findings of any individual study are always open to dispute: for instance, the relative contributions of social class and intelligence to health are genuinely difficult to tease apart.

All of this is subject to vigorous and scholarly debate in the scientific literature, but some opponents of IQ testing, often driven by political concerns, have been far less fair. The most famous of these opponents was the palaeontologist Stephen Jay Gould, who wrote *The Mismeasure of Man* in 1981. This book, which was updated in 1996, is a sustained historical critique of early intelligence research followed by a criticism of factor analysis and the idea of general intelligence.

It is a very partial summary of the literature, omitting opposing data that were readily available at the time of writing. Moreover, researchers doing a follow-up study (Lewis et al., 2011) have found that Gould's conclusions about the accuracy of historical work on head size were simply incorrect. Unfortunately, the book was widely read and, despite now being well out of date, it still has a baleful influence over the IQ debate. There are many others: interested readers should investigate the works of long-time IQ critics such as Leon Kamin and Steven Rose, and see for themselves how their arguments stack up against the scientific research recounted in this book.

This is not, of course, to absolve IQ researchers of any blame: there have been many misleading arguments from a *pro*-IQ perspective, with some researchers – undoubtedly with their own political agendas – making grand, sweeping claims about society and history on the basis of very thin data on intelligence (one example is described by Wicherts et al., 2012). All of this adds up to a very unsatisfying debate: IQ critics often write off intelligence testing on the basis of this minority of slipshod work, leaving the vast majority of sensible scientists, and their painstakingly collected data, standing on the sidelines.

▶ Why study intelligence?

A common question I'm asked when giving public talks or lectures about intelligence is: 'Why do we need to know any of this stuff? What's the point of researching differences in people's intelligence?' There are many answers to this, and a number of them have popped up throughout the book. The simplest one is: 'because intelligence is real, and if we don't research it, we're missing out on an important fact about psychology'. Nevertheless, in the interests of being fully explicit, here are four good reasons (among many) to do intelligence research.

Reason 1

The first reason is the link between intelligence and health. Just looking back at Figure 3.2, which shows the impressive relation between IQ score and mortality risk, should convince you that intelligence is highly relevant in a medical context. We need to know how we can use results from cognitive epidemiology to improve people's health. As discussed by Deary et al. (2010), this might be done by targeting interventions at people according to their level of intelligence, or simply by learning the things that people high in intelligence do, and encouraging others to copy them.

Reason 2

The second reason is the effect of ageing. The make-up of Western society is shifting towards a higher proportion of older people. We saw in Chapter 2 that one of the most striking findings about intelligence is the decline that occurs in its 'fluid' aspects. We also saw that this becomes particularly problematic in old age, when it leads to poorer decision-making and a loss of independence. Intelligence is very stable across life, but it is not unchangeable: finding the factors that might help us preserve our thinking skills into later life is a matter of urgency. Knowing the specific ways in which the brain deteriorates in old age will help us design medicines and treatments to lessen the impact of ageing. Knowing the genetic make-up of intelligence, and which genes (such as *APOE*, discussed in Chapter 4) might predispose us to steeper old-age decline, will allow us more precisely to target our treatments and interventions. This kind of research will also help us understand the diseases of cognitive ageing, like Alzheimer's, that play havoc with mental abilities.

Reason 3

The third reason is the societal importance of intelligence. As I argued in Chapter 3, being bright will be ever more crucial as we get further into the technologized, computerized twenty-first century. Finding ways to truly boost people's intellectual skills, perhaps using the more promising methods we talked about in Chapter 5, will help society, and individuals, to prosper. We can only know how to do this through more intelligence research.

Relatedly, universities, businesses and other employers are always going to want to use ability tests in their admissions and recruitment. We need intelligence research to know how to create tests that aren't biased against particular groups in society, and do the job that historical researchers like Godfrey Thomson wanted them to do: select the most able people, regardless of social class or other advantages. Intelligence research can help us to identify the most talented people who'll foster the artistic and scientific innovation that drives society forwards. At the other end of the spectrum, a deeper knowledge about the nature of general intelligence, and how to measure it, can only be beneficial for diagnosing and helping people with intellectual disabilities.

Reason 4

The final reason is less practical, but no less significant: scientific curiosity. Intelligence is one of the foremost parts of what makes us human: knowing exactly what it is, how it's instantiated in the brain and DNA, and what effects it has on people's lives is part of understanding the story of our species. Variation in intelligence is a subject we all have questions about. Why are some people, even people with similar social backgrounds, so much smarter than others? What caused the genius of Mahler, of Dalí, of Joyce, and of Curie? How can we nurture more geniuses in the future? There is even, dare I say it, something a little poetic about intelligence research: scientists across the world are applying their own intelligence to unravel the mysteries of cognition and the brain.

▶ Conclusion

Intelligence shouldn't be so controversial. We've seen in this final chapter that most of the debate surrounding intelligence stems from some basic misunderstandings of the research. The facts about IQ don't justify unfairness, and nor do they mean that everyone is stuck for ever with the same ability to think and learn. They do have important implications, but we can only consider these if we carefully consider the science. Thankfully, you don't have to look too far to find first-rate intelligence research; I hope I've given some useful pointers in this book.

The political and moral (but usually evidence-free) debate around intelligence distracts from the truly interesting questions. What causes the general factor of intelligence? Which specific genes make a person smarter? Why, exactly, do these seemingly simple tests relate to so many important things in life? What, precisely, is happening in the brain when it's working through an IQ test? How can we make it do that more efficiently? Lately, the field of intelligence research has been buzzing with intriguing new results that begin to address these questions. We can ignore these results, and continue to pretend that intelligence tests are a discredited remnant of psychology's past. Or we can engage with them, and uncover the science of what makes us differ in this most human of attributes. I suspect the latter is the intelligent thing to do.

This 100 ideas section gives ways you can explore the subject in more depth. It's much more than just the usual reading list.

100 IDEAS

Fifteen books about intelligence

1   *IQ and Human Intelligence*, 2nd edition (2011) by Nicholas Mackintosh. An authoritative and balanced textbook and the obvious next step after reading an introductory book like the one you're holding.

2   *Human Intelligence* (2012) by Earl Hunt. Another textbook: an amusing and opinionated journey into the details of intelligence research.

3   *Looking Down on Human Intelligence: From Psychometrics to the Brain* (2000) by Ian J. Deary. Brimming with details and critiques that you won't find elsewhere.

4   *Behavioral Genetics*, 6th edition (2013) by Robert Plomin, John C. DeFries, Valerie S. Knopik and Jenae M. Neiderhiser. The essential textbook on genetics as it relates to intelligence and other psychological traits.

5   *How Intelligence Happens* (2010) by John Duncan. A cognitive neuroscientist tells the story of a lifetime in intelligence research.

6   *Human Cognitive Abilities* (1993) by John B. Carroll. A massive review study in book form, providing incontrovertible evidence for the g-factor.

7   *Bias in Mental Testing* (1983) by Arthur Jensen. One of the most prominent (and controversial) intelligence researchers of the twentieth century asks whether IQ tests are biased against certain groups.

8   *What is Intelligence?* (2009) by James R. Flynn. The Flynn Effect was named for the author of this thoughtful meditation on cognitive ability.

9   *The Bell Curve* (1994) by Richard Herrnstein and Charles Murray. Almost synonymous with 'racism' in some people's minds, but worth reading to understand the debate.

100 Ideas

10 *The Intelligence Men: Makers of the IQ Controversy* (1985) by Raymond E. Fancher. The parts about genetics are now out of date, but this has never been bettered as a historical sketch of Galton, Binet and the other originators of IQ testing.

11 *The Blank Slate: The Modern Denial of Human Nature* (2003) by Steven Pinker. Not strictly about intelligence, but should be read by everyone thinking about the meaning of genetic influences on our psychology.

12 *What Intelligence Tests Miss: The Psychology of Rational Thought* (2009) by Keith E. Stanovich. The confrontational title makes it sound like an anti-IQ book (see below), but really it's a worthwhile read on why intelligent people can sometimes be so irrational.

13 *Sex Differences in Cognitive Abilities*, 4th edition (2013) by Diane S. Halpern. An expert guide through the research on this highly controversial question.

14 *Hereditary Genius* (1869) by Francis Galton. In many ways, the book that started off intelligence research, along with...

15 *The Abilities of Man* (1927), by Charles Spearman. The discoverer of the *g*-factor theorizes about general and specific mental abilities.

Five websites for the latest on intelligence research

Five commonly used intelligence tests

100 Ideas

Twenty intelligence researchers working today and their research areas

26 Camilla P. Benbow, Vanderbilt University (very high intelligence)

27 David Lubinski, Vanderbilt University (very high intelligence)

28 Thomas J. Bouchard, Jr., University of Minnesota (genetics of intelligence)

29 Avshalom Caspi, Duke University (development of intelligence)

30 Stephen J. Ceci, Cornell University (development of intelligence, sex differences)

31 Ian J. Deary, University of Edinburgh (cognitive ageing and cognitive epidemiology)

32 Douglas K. Detterman (learning disabilities)

33 James R. Flynn, University of Otago (rising intelligence)

34 Linda S. Gottfredson, University of Delaware (intelligence and life outcomes)

35 Richard J. Haier, University of California, Irvine (neuroscience of intelligence)

36 Diane Halpern, Claremont McKenna College (sex differences in intelligence)

37 James J. Heckman, University of Chicago (early investment to improve intelligence)

38 Rex E. Jung, University of New Mexico (neuroscience and creativity)

100 Ideas

Ten review papers you should read

46 'Intelligence' (2012) by Ian J. Deary (*Annual Review of Psychology* 63, 453–82) – an excellent overview of recent research, with more book recommendations.

47 'Genes, evolution, and intelligence' (2014) by Thomas J. Bouchard Jr. (*Behavior Genetics*, 44(6), 549–77) – anyone interested in the intelligence of non-human animals, and how it relates to our own, should read this paper.

48 'The neuroscience of human intelligence differences' (2010) by Lars Penke, Wendy Johnson and Ian J. Deary (*Nature Reviews Neuroscience*, 11(3), 201–11) – currently the best summary of the neuroscience of intelligence.

49 'Why *g* matters: The complexity of everyday life' (1997) by Linda S. Gottfredson (*Intelligence*, 24(1), 79–131) – life is an IQ test, and this very practical paper explains why.

50 'Intelligence: Knowns and Unknowns' (1996) by Ulric Neisser et al. (*American Psychologist*, 51(2), 77–101) – a task force of scientists outlines the consensus on intelligence.

51 'Intelligence: New findings and theoretical developments' (2012) by Richard E. Nisbett and colleagues (*American Psychologist*, 67(2), 130–59) – much too strident in places, but a worthwhile description of some recent IQ controversies.

52 'Genetics and intelligence differences: Five special findings' (2014) by Robert Plomin and Ian J. Deary (*Molecular Psychiatry*, 20, 98–108) – an up-to-date and fascinating discussion of the genetics of intelligence.

53 'The processing-speed theory of adult age differences in cognition' (1996) by Timothy A. Salthouse (*Psychological Review*, 103(3), 403–28) – the most comprehensive statement of the theory that cognitive ageing is caused by the brain slowing down.

54 'Scientific and social significance of assessing individual differences: "Sinking shafts at a few points"' (2000) by David Lubinski (*Annual Review of Psychology*, 51, 405–44) – a discussion of how intelligence links with other individual differences to affect our lives.

55 'The validity and utility of selection methods in personnel psychology: Practical and theoretical implications of 85 years of research findings' (1998) by Frank L. Schmidt and John E. Hunter (*Psychological Bulletin*, 124(2), 262–74) – the classic, go-to review of the research on intelligence and occupation.

Five (perhaps) surprising things that correlate with higher intelligence

56 Committing fewer crimes (Moffitt et al., 1994)

57 Having stronger hand grip (Deary et al., 2011)

58 Being taller (Marioni et al., 2014)

59 'Liking' *The Godfather* on Facebook (Kosinski et al., 2013)

60 Making funnier jokes (Greengross and Miller, 2012)

Five historical intelligence researchers not in Chapter 1

61 Raymond B. Cattell (originator of the concepts of 'fluid' and 'crystallized' intelligence)

62 Hans J. Eysenck (heavily involved in the 'nature–nurture' controversy)

63 William Stern (coined the phrase 'intelligence quotient')

64 Louis L. Thurstone (made many statistical contributions)

65 Philip E. Vernon (made major contributions to our understanding of *g*)

Five anti-IQ books

66 *The Mismeasure of Man*, revised and expanded (1996), by Stephen Jay Gould. Beautifully written, as all his books are. But it's at odds with the science and suffers from political bias.

67 *The Science and Politics of IQ* (1974) by Leon J. Kamin. A rather desperate effort to deny any genetic influence on IQ; wrong at the time, and now very outdated.

68 *Multiple Intelligences: New Horizons in Theory and Practice*, completely revised and updated (2006), by Howard Gardner. Loved by teachers but not by scientists.

69 *IQ: A Smart History of a Failed Idea* (2007) by Stephen Murdoch. A strange attempt to smear contemporary intelligence research with the perceived (and sometimes overstated) sins of historical figures.

70 *Intelligence and How to Get It: Why Schools and Cultures Count* (2010) by Richard E. Nisbett. Not anti-IQ per se, but reaches many conclusions that are in conflict with the behaviour–genetic consensus on, for instance, heritability.

Ten common myths (debunked in this book)

71 'You can't sum up a person/measure a person's worth in a single number.' (Nobody said you could – see Chapter 3.)

72 'Intelligence tests only tell you how good you are at doing intelligence tests.' (They tell you much more than that – see Chapter 3.)

73 'Your IQ is just a reflection of your social background.' (IQ only correlates modestly with social background – see Chapter 3.)

74 'There are multiple separate intelligences.' (All mental abilities are correlated – see Chapter 2.)

75 'Brain size isn't related to intelligence.' (Larger brains are linked to higher IQ – see Chapter 4.)

76 'Intelligence is immutable.' (There's plenty of evidence for IQ change – see Chapter 5.)

77 'Intelligence research is elitist/sexist/racist.' (Facts don't have moral values attached – see Chapter 6.)

78 'Intelligence tests just measure culturally valued information.' (They include much more basic tests, like speed – see Chapter 2.)

79 'Twin studies have been discredited.' (They haven't, and even if they had, other methods tell us that IQ is heritable – see Chapter 4.)

80 'IQ tests were originally invented for eugenic purposes.' (The story is complex, but the first test was invented by Binet to help children with learning disabilities – see Chapter 1.)

Five fictional characters known for high intelligence...

81 Tony Stark (*Iron Man*)

82 Marvin the Paranoid Android (*Hitchhiker's Guide to the Galaxy*)

83 Ozymandias (*Watchmen*)

84 Odysseus (*The Odyssey*)

85 Ivan Karamazov (*The Brothers Karamazov*)

...and five known for low intelligence

86 Lenny (*Of Mice and Men*)

87 Baldrick (*Blackadder*)

88 Homer Simpson (*The Simpsons*)

89 Obelix (*Asterix*)

90 Inspector Clouseau (*The Pink Panther*)

Ten 'big questions' for future intelligence research

91 What exactly is the *g*-factor? Was Spearman correct, or was Thomson?

92 How do we combine structural and functional brain imaging to understand intelligence?

93 What are the specific genes or genetic mutations that affect IQ, and where in the brain do they have their effects?

94 How do genes interact and correlate with different environments to affect intelligence?

95 What exactly is causing the Flynn Effect? Is it slowing down?

96 What is it about education that seems to boost intelligence, and how can we maximize this boost?

97 Are processing speed and working memory fundamental to general intelligence?

98 Why are males more variable in their intelligence than females?

99 Can we design drugs, nutritional interventions or video games that enhance intelligence?

100 How do we prevent cognitive ageing?

References

▶ Chapter 1

Deary, I. J. (2000), *Looking Down on Human Intelligence: From Psychometrics to the Brain* (Oxford: Oxford University Press).

Deary, I. J. (2013), 'An intelligent Scotland: Professor Sir Godfrey Thomson and the Scottish Mental Surveys of 1932 and 1947', *Journal of the British Academy*, 1, 95–131.

Fancher, R. E. (1985), *The Intelligence Men: Makers of the IQ Controversy* (London: Norton).

Galton, F. (1908), *Memories of My Life* (London: Methuen).

Gottfredson, L. S. (1997), 'Mainstream science on intelligence', *Intelligence*, 24(1) 13–23.

Jensen, A. R. (1998), *The g Factor: The Science of Mental Ability* (London: Praeger).

Johnson, R. C. et al. (1985), 'Galton's data a century later', *American Psychologist*, 40(8) 875–92.

Nicolas, S. et al. (2013), 'Sick? Or Slow? On the origins of intelligence as a psychological object', *Intelligence,* 41(5) 699–711.

Pearson, K. (1914), *The Life, Letters and Labours of Francis Galton* (Cambridge: Cambrige University Press).

Yerkes, R. (1921), *Psychological Examining in the United States Army* (Washington DC: Government Printing Office), 256.

▶ Chapter 2

Bartholomew, D. J. et al. (2009), 'A new lease of life for Thomson's bonds model of intelligence', *Psychological Review*, 116(3) 567–79.

Carroll, J. B. (1993), *Human Cognitive Abilities: A Survey of Factor-Analytic Studies* (Cambridge: Cambridge University Press).

Conway, A. R. A. et al. (2003), 'Working memory capacity and its relation to general intelligence', *Trends in Cognitive Sciences*, 7(12) 547–52.

Deary, I. J. (2000), *Looking Down on Human Intelligence: From Psychometrics to the Brain* (Oxford: Oxford University Press).

Deary, I. J. et al. (2013), 'The stability of intelligence from age 11 to age 90 years: The Lothian Birth Cohort of 1921', *Psychological Science*, 24(12) 2361–8.

Gignac, G. A. (2014), 'Dynamic mutualism versus *g* factor theory: An empirical test', *Intelligence*, 42, 89–97.

Jensen, A. R. (2006), *Clocking the Mind: Mental Chronometry and Individual Differences* (Amsterdam: Elsevier).

Johnson, W. and Bouchard, Jr, T. J. (2005), 'The structure of human intelligence: It is verbal, perceptual, and image rotation (VPR), not fluid and crystallized.' *Intelligence*, 33(4) 393–416.

Johnson, W. et al. (2008), 'Still just 1 *g*: Consistent results from five test batteries', *Intelligence*, 36(1) 81–95.

Lövdén, M. et al. (2013), 'Lifestyle change and the prevention of cognitive decline and dementia: what is the evidence?', *Current Opinion in Psychiatry*, 26(3) 239–43.

Tucker-Drob, E. M. (2009), *Developmental Psychology*, 45(5) 1097–118.

Tucker-Drob, E. M. (2011), 'Neurocognitive functions and everyday functions change together in old age', *Neuropsychology*, 25(3) 368–77.

van der Maas, H. L. et al. (2006), 'A dynamical model of general intelligence: The positive manifold of intelligence by mutualism', *Psychological Review*, 113(4) 842–61.

Waterhouse, L. (2006), 'Multiple intelligences, the Mozart Effect, and Emotional Intelligence: A critical review', *Educational Psychologist*, 41(4) 207–25.

▶ Chapter 3

Ali, A. et al. (2013), 'The relationship between happiness and intelligent quotient: The contribution of socio-economic and clinical factors', *Psychological Medicine*, 43(6) 1303–12.

Bates, T. C. (2007), 'Fluctuating asymmetry and intelligence', *Intelligence*, 35(1) 41–6.

Batty, G.D., et al. (2007), 'Premorbid (early life) IQ and later mortality risk: Systematic review', *Annals of Epidemiology*, 17(4), 278–88.

Batty, G. D. et al. (2008), *British Journal of Psychiatry*, 193, 461–5.

Batty, G.D. et al. (2008), 'IQ in early adulthood, socioeconomic position, and unintentional injury mortality by middle age: a cohort study of more than 1 million Swedish men', *Epidemiology*, 20(1) 100–109.

Calvin, C.M. et al. (2010), 'Intelligence in youth and all-cause mortality: Systematic review and meta-analysis', *International Journal of Epidemiology*, 40(3) 626–44.

Carl, N. (2014), 'Verbal intelligence is correlated with socially and economically liberal beliefs', *Intelligence*, 44, 142–8.

Deary, I. J. (2008), 'Why do intelligent people live longer?', *Nature*, 456(7219) 175–6.

Deary, I. J. et al. (2005), 'Intergenerational social mobility and mid-life status attainment: influences of childhood intelligence, childhood social factors, and education', *Intelligence*, 33(5) 455–72.

Deary, I. J. et al. (2007), 'Intelligence and educational achievement', *Intelligence*, 35(1) 13–21.

Deary, I. J. (2008), 'Bright children become enlightened adults', *Psychological Science*, 19(1) 1–6.

Gale, C. R. et al. (2010), 'Intelligence in early adulthood and subsequent hospitalization and admission rates for the whole range of mental disorders: longitudinal study of 1,049,663 men', *Epidemiology*, 21(1) 70–77.

Gale, C. R. et al. (2013), 'Is bipolar disorder more common in highly intelligent people? A cohort study of a million men', *Molecular Psychiatry*, 18(2) 190–94.

Gottfredson, L. S. (2004), 'Intelligence: Is it the epidemiologist's elusive "fundamental cause" of social class inequalities in health?', *Journal of Personality and Social Psychology*, 86(1) 174–99.

Joseph, D. L. and Newman, D. A. (2010), 'Emotional intelligence: An integrative meta-analysis and cascading model', *Journal of Applied Psychology*, 95(1) 54–78.

Kell, H. J. et al. (2013), 'Who rises to the top? Early indicators', *Psychological Science*, 24(5) 648–59.

Kendler, K. S. et al. (2014), 'IQ and schizophrenia in a Swedish national sample: Their causal relationship and the interaction of IQ with genetic risk', *American Journal of Psychiatry*, doi: 10.1176/appi.ajp.2014.14040516.

Kuncel, N. R. and Hezlett, S. A. (2010), *Current Directions in Psychological Science*, 19(6) 339–45.

Marks, G. N. (2014), *Education, Social Background, and Cognitive Ability: The Decline of the Social* (London: Routledge).

Mosing, M.A. et al. (2014), 'Genetic pleiotropy explains associations between musical auditory discrimination and intelligence', *PLoS ONE*, 9(11) e113874.

Nusbaum, E. C. and Silvia, P. J. (2011), 'Are intelligence and creativity really so different? Fluid intelligence, executive processes, and strategy use in divergent thinking', *Intelligence* 36–45.

Ritchie, S. J. and Bates, T. C. (2013), 'Enduring links from childhood mathematics and reading achievement to adult socioeconomic status', *Psychological Science*, 24(7) 1301–8.

Robertson, K. F. et al. (2010), 'Beyond the threshold hypothesis: Even among the gifted and top math/science graduate students, cognitive abilities, vocational interests, and lifestyle preferences matter for career choice, performance, and persistence',*Current Directions in Psychological Science*, 19(6) 346–51.

Strenze, T. (2007), 'Intelligence and socioeconomic success: A meta-analytic review of longitudinal research', *Intelligence*, 35(5) 401–26.

Teasdale, T. W. et al. (1988), 'Degree of myopia in relation to intelligence and educational level', *The Lancet*, 2(8624) 1351–4.

Wai, J. et al. (2005), 'Creativity and Occupational Accomplishments Among Intellectually Precocious Youths: An Age 13 to Age 33 Longitudinal Study', *Journal of Educational Psychology*, 97(3) 484–92.

Wai, J. et al. (2009), 'Spatial ability for STEM domains: Aligning over 50 years of cumulative psychological knowledge solidifies its importance', *Journal of Educational Psychology*, 101(4) 817–35.

Wolf, M. B. and Ackerman, P. L. (2005), 'Extraversion and intelligence: A meta-analytic investigation', *Personality and Individual Differences*, 39(3) 531–42.

Wrulich, M. et al. (2014), 'Forty years on: Childhood intelligence predicts health in middle adulthood', *Health Psychology*, 33(3) 292–6.

Zuckerman, M. et al. (2013), 'The relation between intelligence and religiosity: a meta-analysis and some proposed explanations', *Personality and Social Psychology Review*, 17(4) 325–54.

▶ Chapter 4

Arslan, R. C. et al. (2014), 'The effect of paternal age on offspring intelligence and personality when controlling for paternal trait level', *PLoS ONE*, 9(5) e97370.

Asbury, K. and Plomin, R. (2014), *G is for Genes: The Impact of Genetics on Education and Achievement* (Chichester: Wiley-Blackwell).

Bates, T. C. and Tucker-Drob, E. M. (2014), 'The world's literature on gene x social class interactions on cognitive ability: A meta-analysis', doi: 10.6084/m9.figshare.1275289

Bouchard, Jr., T. J. (2014), 'Genes, evolution, and intelligence', *Behavior Genetics*, 44(6) 549–77.

Chabris, C. F. et al. (2012), 'Most reported genetic associations with general intelligence are probably false positives', *Psychological Science*, 23(11) 1314–23.

Davies, G. et al. (2015), *Molecular Psychiatry*, 20, 183–92.

Davies, G. et al. (2011), 'Genome-wide association studies establish that human intelligence is highly heritable and polygenic', *Molecular Psychiatry*, 16(10) 996–1005.

Duncan, J. (2010), *How Intelligence Happens* (New Haven: Yale University Press).

Harris, J. R. (2009), *The Nurture Assumption: Why Children Turn Out the Way They Do*, 2nd edn (New York: Free Press).

Jung, R. E. and Haier, R. J. (2007), 'The Parieto-Frontal Integration Theory (P-FIT) of intelligence: converging neuroimaging evidence', *Behavioural and Brain Sciences*, 30(2) 135–54.

Krapohl, E. et al. (2014), 'The high heritability of educational achievement reflects many genetically influenced traits, not just intelligence', *Proceedings of the National Academy of Sciences*, 111(42) 15273–8.

Lövdén, M. et al. (2014), 'Changes in perceptual speed and white matter microstructure in the corticospinal tract are associated in very old age', *NeuroImage*, 102, 520–30.

Penke, L. et al. (2012), 'Brain white matter tract integrity as a neural foundation for general intelligence', *Molecular Psychiatry*, 17(10) 1026–30.

Pietschnig, J., *SSRN* (2014), 'Meta-analysis of associations between human brain volume and intelligence differences: How strong are they and what do they mean?', doi: 10.2139/ssrn.2512128.

Pinker, S. (2010), 'The cognitive niche: Coevolution of intelligence, sociality, and language', *Proceedings of the National Academy of Sciences*, 107(2) 8993–9.

Plomin, R. and Deary, I. J. (2014), 'Genetics and intelligence differences: Five special findings', *Molecular Psychiatry* doi: 10.1038/mp.2014.105.

Plomin, R. et al. (1997), 'Nature, nurture, and cognitive development from 1 to 16 years: A parent–offspring adoption study', *Psychological Science*, 8(6) 442–7.

Plomin, R. et al. (2013,) *Behavioral Genetics* (New York: Worth Publishers).

Potts, R. (2011), *Nature*, 480, 43–4.

Schiepers, O. J. G. et al. (2012), 'APOE E4 status predicts age-related cognitive decline in the ninth decade: longitudinal follow-up of the Lothian Birth Cohort 1921', *Molecular Psychiatry*, 17, 315–24.

Shaw, P. et al. (2006), 'Intellectual ability and cortical development in children and adolescents', *Nature*, 440(7084) 676–9.

▶ Chapter 5

Barnett, W. S. (1998), 'Long-term cognitive and academic effects of early childhood education on children in poverty', *Preventative Medicine*, 27(2) 204–7.

Brinch, C. N. and Galloway, T. A. (2012), 'Schooling in adolescence raises IQ scores', *Proceedings of the National Academy of Sciences*, 109(2) 425–30.

Cakic, V. (2009), 'Smart drugs for cognitive enhancement: Ethical and pragmatic considerations in the era of cosmetic neurology', *Journal of Medical Ethics*, 35, 611–5.

Der, G. et al. (2006), 'Effect of breastfeeding on intelligence in children: Prospective study, sibling pairs analysis, and meta-analysis', BMJ, 333, 945.

Ezeamama, A. E. et al. (2012), 'Treatment for *Schistosoma japonicum*, reduction of intestinal parasite load, and cognitive test score improvements in school-aged children', *PLoS Neglected Tropical Diseases*, 6(5) e1634.

Flynn, J. R. (2012), *Are We Getting Smarter? Rising IQ in the Twenty-first Century* (Cambridge: Cambridge University Press).

Huang, P.-C. et al. (2012), 'Childhood blood lead levels and intellectual development after ban of leaded gasoline in Taiwan: a 9-year prospective study', *Environment International*, 40, 88–96.

Jaeggi, S. M. et al. (2008), 'Improving fluid intelligence with training on working memory', *Proceedings of the National Academy of Sciences*, 105(19) 6829–33.

Karbach, J. and Verhaeghen, P. (2014), 'Making working memory work: A meta-analysis of executive-control and working memory training in older adults', *Psychological Science*, 25(11) 2027–37.

Kennedy, D. O. et al. (2009), 'Cognitive and mood effects of 8 weeks' supplementation with 400 mg or 1000 mg of the omega-3 essential fatty acid docosahexaenoic acid (DHA) in healthy children aged 10–12 years', *Nutritional Neuroscience*, 12(2) 48–56.

Melby-Lervåg, M. and Hulme, C. (2013), 'Is working memory training effective? A meta-analytic review', *Developmental Psychology*, 49(2) 270–91.

Mortensen, E. L. et al. (2002), 'The association between duration of breastfeeding and adult intelligence', *JAMA*, 287(18) 2365–71.

Nettelbeck, T. and Wilson, C. (2004), 'The Flynn Effect: Smarter not faster', *Intelligence*, 32(1) 85–93.

Pietschnig, J. et al. (2010), 'Mozart effect-Schmozart effect. A meta-analysis', *Intelligence*, 38(3) 314–23.

Puma, M. et al. (2010), *Head Start Impact Study: Final Report* (Washington, DC: US Department of Health and Human Services).

Qian, M. et al. (2005), 'The effects of iodine on intelligence in children: a meta-analysis of studies conducted in China', *Asia Pacific Journal of Clinical Nutrition*, 14(1) 32–42.

Rauscher, F. et al. (1993), 'Music and spatial task performance', *Nature*, 365(6447) 611.

Trahan, L. H. et al. (2014), 'The Flynn Effect: A meta-analysis', *Psychological Bulletin*, 140(5) 1332–60.

Walfisch, A. et al. (2013), 'Breast milk and cognitive development – the role of confounders: A systematic review', *BMJ Open*, 3(8) e003259.

Wongupparaj, P. et al. (2015), 'A cross-temporal meta-analysis of Raven's Progressive Matrices: Age groups and developing versus developed countries', *Intelligence*, 49, 1–9.

▶ Chapter 6

Boliver, V., and Swift, A. (2011), 'Do comprehensive schools reduce social mobility?', *British Journal of Sociology*, 61(1) 89–110.

Deary, I. J. et al. (2010), 'Intelligence and personality as predictors of illness and death: How researchers in differential psychology and chronic disease epidemiology are collaborating to understand and address health inequalities', *Psychological Science in the Public Interest* 11(2) 53–79.

Gould, S. J. (1996), *The Mismeasure of Man,* revised edn (New York: Norton).

Herrnstein, R. J., and Murray, C. (1994), *The Bell Curve: Intelligence and Class Structure in American Life* (New York: Free Press).

Hunt, E. and Carlson, J. (2007), 'Considerations relating to the study of group differences in intelligence', *Perspectives on Psychological Science*, 2(2) 194–213.

Jensen, A. R. (1969), 'How much can we boost IQ and scholastic achievement?', *Harvard Educational Review*, 39(1) 1–123.

Johnson, W. et al. (2008), 'Sex differences in variability in general intelligence: A new look at the old question', *Perspectives on Psychological Science*, 3(6) 518–31.

Lewis, J. E. et al. (2011), 'The mismeasure of science: Stephen Jay Gould versus Samuel George Morton on skulls and bias', *PLoS Biology*, 9(6) e1001071.

Mackintosh, N. J. (2011), *IQ and Human Intelligence* (Oxford: Oxford University Press).

Miller, D. I. and Halpern, D. F. (2014), 'The new science of cognitive sex differences', *Trends in Cognitive Sciences*, 18(1) 37–45.

Nisbett, R. E. (2010), *Intelligence and How to Get It: Why Schools and Cultures Count* (New York: Norton).

Pinker, S. (2002), *The Blank Slate: The Modern Denial of Human Nature* (London: Penguin).

Proctor, R. N. (2000), *The Nazi War on Cancer* (Princeton, NJ: Princeton University Press).

Singer, P. (1995), *Animal Liberation* (London: Pimlico).

Wicherts, J. M. et al. (2012), 'Letting the daylight in: Reviewing the reviewers and other ways to maximize transparency in science', *Frontiers in Computational Neuroscience*, 6, 20.

▶ 100 Ideas

Deary, I. J. et al. (2011), 'Losing one's grip: a bivariate growth curve model of grip strength and nonverbal reasoning from age 79 to 87 years in the Lothian Birth Cohort 1921', *The Journals of Gerontology, Series B*, 66B(6) 699–707.

Greengross, G. and Miller, G. (2011), 'Humor ability reveals intelligence, predicts mating success, and is higher in males', *Intelligence*, 39(4) 188–92.

Kosinski, M. et al. (2013), 'Private traits and attributes are predictable from digital records of human behavior', *Proceedings of the National Academy of Sciences*, 110(15) 5802–5.

Marioni, R. E. et al. (2014), 'Common genetic variants explain the majority of the correlation between height and intelligence: The Generation Scotland Study', *Behavior Genetics*, 44, 91–6.

Moffitt, T. E. et al. (1994) *Criminology*, 'Neuropsychological tests predicting persistent male delinquency', 32(2) , 277–300.

Index

Also available in the series

Ziauddin Sardar

MUHAMMAD

BIOETHICS

Donna Dickenson

Julian Baggini

PHILOSOPHY

GOD

Mark Vernon

JUDAISM

Keith Kahn-Harris

LOVE

Mark Vernon

WATER

Paul Younger

Richard Huxtable

EUTHANASIA

Pascale F. Engelmajer

BUDDHISM

Andrew Silke

TERRORISM

HUMAN RIGHTS

Ivan Fiser

Johanna Oksala

POLITICAL PHILOSOPHY

Chris Goodall

SUSTAINABILITY

Alastair J.L. Blanshard

CLASSICAL WORLD

Mark Rowlands

ANIMAL RIGHTS

DEMOCRACY

Steven Beller

Samantha Lyle

Tim Hall

David Ashford

John Manley

Barry Kemp

Jonathan Clements

Michael Scott

Michael Scott

Peter Warren &
Michael Streeter

Ken Booth

Ziauddin Sardar

Michael Halvorson

Lorna Selfe

Ieuan Williams

Camilla Ween

Sandi Mann

Picture credits

Figure 1.1: Plate lxi from K. Pearson, *The Life, Letters, and Labours of Francis Galton* (Cambridge, Cambridge University Press, 1914), available at http://www.galton.org

Figure 1.2: Image from R. Yerkes, *Psychological Examining in the United States Army* (Washington, DC: Government Printing Office, 1921), p. 256

Figure 4.3: Image courtesy of Mark Bastin, The University of Edinburgh

Figure 5.1: Image adapted from Wongupparaj et al. 2015, with permission from Elsevier.

All That Matters books are written by the world's leading experts, to introduce the most exciting and relevant areas of an important topic to students and general readers.

From Bioethics to Muhammad and Philosophy to Sustainability, the *All That Matters* series covers the most controversial and engaging topics from science, philosophy, history, religion and other fields. The authors are world-class academics or top public intellectuals, on a mission to bring the most interesting and challenging areas of their subject to new readers.

Each book contains a unique '100 ideas' section, giving inspiration to readers whose interest has been piqued and who want to explore the subject further. Find out more, at:

www.allthatmattersbooks.com
Facebook/allthatmattersbooks
Twitter@_JMLearning